All 'Beings' Are of Equal Value –

Consciousness and the Pursuit of Excellence

In Service to Self and In Service to All Beings

– A Blueprint for the New Societies of a New Consciousness

New Energy Civilization

Second Edition

EPub   ISBN: 978-0-6487633-0-7

Mobi   ISBN: 978-0-6487633-1-4

Paperback ISBN: 978-0-6487633-2-1

Hardcover ISBN: 978-0-6487633-3-8

Cover:

Planetary images – courtesy of NASA Images:
NASA/Ames/JPL-Caltech
TrES-2b: Dark Planet Illustration Credit: David A. Aguilar (CfA), TrES, Kepler, NASA
NASA/NOAA/GSFC/Suomi NPP/VIIRS/Norman Kuring
Kepler 47b & 47c: NASA/JPL-Caltech/T. Pyle
NASA/JPL-Caltech/R. Hurt
NASA Ames Research Center/W. Stenzel

Background – my photo of Uluru, Northern Territory, Australia. The pixilated nature of my front and back cover photos attempts to show that everything in creation is composed of vibrating particles of Consciousness energies and that reality is fluid.

Ibironke Lardner
Horation Ink Publishing
horation_ink@internode.on.net

Table of Contents

DEDICATION

To my sister, Tunday, who was the first in the family to start questioning reality and so set all of us off in search of answers.

To my sister Buky (Zanubia), whose job in a bookshop enabled her to access literature that provided some wonderful signposts and so set all of us off on an incredible quest for our own enlightenment.

To my brother, Jiday, for all his love and unwavering support over the years.

To my sister Dupeh for all her loving support.

To my Mother and Father – thank you.

To Bill, who brilliantly played the role he had to play in order to get me to this point.

To my beloved children, Patricia and William, who sometimes worried that I had lost my marbles but who didn't see symptoms that were enough to make them scared and call the family doctor!

To Jean Tinder, who helped me to truly see with more than just my eyes!

And to me, for fulfilling a promise to the Ancient Ones, the Spiritual Elders, by returning to Uluru (Northern Territory, Australia), that wonderful and blessed Rock of Ages, to bring blessings and receive blessings.

FOREWORD

This Blueprint is a simple description of my vision for the creation of the New Societies of a New Consciousness New Energy Civilization (also simply referred to as *New Consciousness Civilization* in this book), based on the principles of my spiritual viewpoint, which I have entitled *All 'Beings' Are of Equal Value: Consciousness and the Pursuit of Excellence In Service to Self and In Service to All Beings.'*

The advent of the human race on Earth required the creation and establishment of duality – the dance of polar opposites: yin yang, hot cold, hard soft, light dark, etc. – to act as a catalyst for human growth and evolution, with money, its inseparable Siamese-twin, power, and religion being the three most powerful and effective tools employed by humans to establish, maintain and sustain this dual state of being.

These tools have performed brilliantly and done exactly what they were meant to do – take human civilization on its current foundations as far as it can go. But there are now clear signs that through the continued use of these tools, particularly money and power, humanity is struggling to maintain its balance.

It is said that civilisation, like the sun, rises in the East and sets in the West. I believe that many would agree that we are now in the midst of a setting and that current ideologies, systems and structures are now, in many ways, failing to serve humanity. From the spiritual point of view, there are many who desire to experience all the struggles and other manifestations of a civilization come full circle, as it is important for their spiritual growth and evolution.

However, there are many others who are in a different space and place and who see this period of change as an opportunity to make a long-prophesied quantum leap, as human consciousness breaks through the barriers of civilization as it has been lived and experienced up to the present, and through the grandest of adventures spins off into states-of-being as yet unknown to man.

The philosophy of *All 'Beings' Are of Equal Value: Consciousness and the Pursuit of Excellence In Service to Self and In Service to All Beings* is that, as a Being birthed by God The Creator The Eternal Infinite Living Void of Consciousness, **you are God Also and Co-creator of life, the Earth, the Universe and Creation. As God Also, all Beings are created equal and are valuable beyond measure. As such, all Beings are of the same value and therefore, All 'Beings' Are of Equal Value.**

With this understanding comes the realization that, indeed, there is no Divine Law anywhere that proclaims that humanity must forevermore make use of the artificial medium of money. We can progress from using this artificial medium to give artificial values to anyone and to define most things in society.

As such, Human Beings do not need money in order to survive, thrive and evolve. Human Beings can now let go of money – can now take money out of the equation! Humans can now allow the Divine energy that manifests as money to also break out of its boundaries, release itself from its current form, and be transmuted to Divine Life Force energies that can be brought back down to Earth by humans, to serve humanity in totally new and different ways.

Ergo a New Consciousness New Energy Civilization based on the principle that **All 'Beings' Are of Equal Value, where money and all its related systems, structures, institutions and values cease to exist. A New Consciousness Civilization in which the current unrelenting pursuit of profit, as well as all the other money-based values that underpin human civilization and motivate human society today, are replaced by a new Standard: The Pursuit of Excellence In Service to Self and In Service to All Beings, thereby creating a civilization where the governing of a country is truly of the people, by the people, for the people.** A civilization **of sophisticated simplicity** where, instead of spending their lives serving and conforming to processes, systems, structures and technology, and to governments that spend an inordinate amount of time and energy dictating and enforcing levels of poverty on their citizens, humanity's constant striving for a higher consciousness and a deeper awareness, ensures that **processes, systems, structures and in particular, technology, are put in place purely to serve all Beings and enable them to live a life of ease and grace.**

I am among many who genuinely believe that there are other dignified and humane ways to live and who are happy to think outside the box and go on an adventure in order to discover what those other ways could be.

For those who choose to go on this adventure, the foundation and fundamentals of civilization as we have known them begin to slip away as we transition from the old to the new, to be replaced by new realities that give human consciousness the space and the impetus to go on grand adventures of discovery and in the process birth a New Consciousness New Energy Civilization.

I hope this blueprint is a source of inspiration!

Ibironke Lardner

spiriturealities@gmail.com

www.spiriturealities.com

&

allbeingsareequal@gmail.com

www.allbeingsareequal.com

1

CONSCIOUSNESS, HIGHER PASSION AND THE GRACE OF GNOST

Following on from my Foreword, my aim in this first chapter is to lay out the spiritual tenets that form the foundation upon which my concept for a New Consciousness New Energy Civilization is built.

The whole of original Creation has often been described as a Void; an unformed vastness; one could even say a No-thing-ness. But Nothingness or a Void has to exist in order to be a Void or Nothingness. They have to be in a State-of- Being in order to be Nothingness or a Void. To exist, to be, requires that you have life; and to have life means that you are aware, that you are conscious. Life is Awareness, which is Consciousness and so a Void or

Nothingness carried within itself consciousness of its state-of-Being as Nothingness or a Void.

Therefore, consciousness is innate to and inseparable from Nothingness/a Void. There has to be some part somewhere in Nothingness that is aware; that is conscious. You can only know something as something because you become aware of it. You can only know nothing as nothing, or a void as a void because you become aware of it as nothing; as a void; as something! In order for you to become aware of anything at all, you have to be conscious. You could say that consciousness calls things into existence in your reality. Yet, in order for you to be conscious, you have to exist and when you become aware of yourself as existing, is when you initiate recognition and can then also initiate action, reaction and interaction.

And so it is that everything, including a void and nothing, is a *state-of-being*, or is *in-a-state-of-being*. As stated earlier, for anything to 'be', for anything to exist, it has to have life; it has to be alive, no matter in how basic or simple a manner; and it would be safe to say, that as far as we all can perceive, there is nothing in Creation that is not alive or that has no life force – an in-breath and an out-breath, a pulse or some sort of movement, no matter how shallow, minuscule or imperceptible. Therefore, to be alive also means being live, that is to say being active, being aware, capable of recognizing and capable of *knowing*.

And so it is, that this state of being of a void had to be a living thing in order to be, in order to exist, and this grand living Nothingness is, in my view, primordial

Consciousness and was and is the primordial source of the substance of all Creation. I most humbly and respectfully call this Consciousness, *God The Creator The Eternal Infinite Living Void of Consciousness*, from and by Whom all Beings and all States-of-Being have been and are created, be they animate or inanimate, solid or ethereal.

Therefore: State of Being/Existing/Living = Life/Alive/Live/Motion = Awareness = Consciousness = State of Being/Existing/Living = Life/Alive/Live/Motion = Awareness = Consciousness = State of Being/. . . a circle with no beginning and no end.

And so, God The Creator The Eternal Infinite Living Void of Consciousness, whom I will also simply call Creator Eternal Infinite, simply just forever **Was**; simply just forever **Is**.

And so it is that the Creation story, which together with the game of opposites that we call Duality, form the matrix within which human beings are to create, experience, grow and evolve, states that Creator Eternal Infinite sought to know all of Itself; sought to experience all of Itself by having the feeling-thought, "Who Am I?"

Feeling-thought because the following suddenly dawned on me about thoughts and feelings: Feeling is a state-of-being; but I also suddenly realized that even a thought is a state-of-being; it exists and therefore it is a living thing. Thoughts are produced by living Beings and, once thought, they continue to exist because thoughts are alive. From my layman's observation, thought and feeling are the two sides of the same coin, as more often than not, thoughts seem to arise from some sort of feeling – whether it is one of curiosity, a desire to know, a desire to make

sense of something, a desire to express something, a desire to express movement, to act, etc. Even a lack of empathy is a feeling. A thought is therefore imbued with feeling and precisely because of that, a thought, once thought, becomes a living thing and is live, it can be re-thought, remembered, expanded, built upon, changed, and its purpose can be manifested.

This feeling-thought by Creator Eternal Infinite to know Itself, to me, proves beyond any shadow of a doubt that Creator Eternal Infinite, at a minimum, has to be alive, has to have awareness and the capacity to know, has to have feeling, in some form or another, in order to express such a desire to know Itself. It was a feeling-thought so profound that it resulted in tremendous acts of self-expression, that modified and transformed the very structure of the pure Creator Eternal Infinite Consciousness of these acts, into **Divine Life Forces** that created the very first forms of Created Creation. One could describe these Divine Life Forces as Creator Eternal Infinite In Action.

For, I think we all generally agree that pure Creator Eternal Infinite Consciousness is formless. The way I see it, therefore, is that any extrusions of this pure Consciousness into any type of form, instantly steps down the vibration and modifies the structure of this pure Consciousness into a denser form of Consciousness – which I call Divine Life Force.

And so began the stupendous creation of Created Creation, with Creator Eternal Infinite projecting Itself, in the form of Divine Life Forces, from, into and within Its own pure body of Consciousness, creating in myriad endless ways, putting boundaries around each one in order to enable each creation to become, and hold itself together as, a separate entity.

God The Creator The Eternal Infinite Living Void of Consciousness birthed the *Creator Gods* – the Nebulae/Nebulas who created the universes. *MotherFatherSource*, the Creator God of our Universe within which our Galaxy and our World sits, birthed the *Creator Beings*, who then projected physical Aspects of themselves as human and other Beings here on Earth. Other Creator Gods did likewise, projecting themselves in myriad other forms into physical and non-physical realities elsewhere in Creation.

Now, at this point let me clarify that this is my very simple understanding of Creation that I am stating here above and here below.

It goes without saying that between Creator Eternal Infinite and the Creator Gods, between the Creator Gods and the Creator Beings, and between the Creator Beings and their Expressions in physical and non-physical Worlds, there are countless levels and forms of existence, as Creator Eternal Infinite Consciousness is stepped down in form, complexity and density to arrive at the level of the human and similar or even denser forms of Expression.

As I understand it, the human is still capable of using Consciousness to independently create, experience, grow and evolve to become a Divine Creator because Creator

Eternal Infinite's Pure Consciousness is embodied by the human in the form of the *I AM Presence,* the God Spark that sits within and yet encompasses the Spirit/Light/Etheric/ and other Bodies that make up the human being.

But beyond this simple depiction, I shall not worry myself to go because this is enough to enable me to function; to keep on going! I believe that when a human Being gets to the point where they begin to experience the same feeling-thought of "Who Am I?" they tap into Divine Consciousness that provides them with information, that enables them to have enough of an idea that makes sense to their senses, at their level of understanding; an understanding that the human can work with and that enables them to keep on going, rather than grind to a halt and get stuck going round and round in circles for ages in their spiritual growth. So, what I am writing here is the information I have tapped into and channelled, and I eagerly and proudly work with it.

God The Creator The Eternal Infinite Living Void of Consciousness, and as Its Expression, Creator God MotherFatherSource, forever have the infinite and eternal capacity to endure and to nurture all Beings in all States-of-Being as they are conceived, or created, or take form, or manifest, or unfold, grow, evolve and reach their totality of being, finite or infinite, no matter how long this takes or endures. And that is the Love that is Creator Eternal Infinite, expressed through all of Creation.

Here, let me explain the meaning of *Being* and *State-of-Being*.

A *Being* is you and I and all forms of life. It is whatever **form** that Creator Eternal Infinite chooses to incarnate in, whether animate or inanimate, physical or ethereal, eg. a Creator God, a Creator Being, a human life form, life forms that are alien/unfamiliar/unknown to humans, a rock, trees, sand, water, wind, mountains, ants, a butterfly.

State-of-Being is, first and foremost, *existing*, it is *being*; and then it refers to the **manner** in which a Being chooses to exist, chooses to be, chooses to live, chooses to become, to grow, to evolve. It refers to the reality a Being chooses to create, in which to experience their existence, in which to experience their Divine purpose, in which to experience their creativity, in which to experience their life moment by moment.

As expressions of Creator Eternal Infinite, all 'Beings' that constitute Created Creation embody Creator Eternal Infinite's passion to fully know themselves and the rest of Creation. As an expression of Creator God MotherFatherSource, I Am ultimately also an expression of Creator Eternal Infinite's passion to know Itself empirically: *'I exist! . . . But . . .hmmm . . . Who Am I?!'* I therefore also embody that same passion to fully know myself and to know Creation.

And how do I do that? In the same way Creator Eternal Infinite did and does: by expressing my passion through the act of creating and then immersing myself in my creations, to experience them.

So, how do we create?

I am one of those who feel that if something actually happens on the Godly/celestial/cosmic/spiritual/etheric/you-know-what-I-mean realms, that then manifests in reality, then there is a way by which it happens that can be known and understood. And I *sooooo* want to know and understand how, as best I can! I need to know and understand how it happens, as best I can! I find it very difficult to engage with something I do not at all understand; I do not know *how* to engage with something I do not at all understand; that I do not have even the most basic, the most rudimentary understanding about. In those instances, I either park the issue to the side, forget about it and move on – something hard to do – or, more often than not, I obsess about it and worry and worry and question and question until I at least arrive at a rudimentary understanding. In the early days of my awakening and walking my spiritual path, this could take anything from days to years.

Let me repeat here what I said earlier. This is my very simple understanding of Creation that I am stating in this treatise; an understanding that makes sense to my senses and that I can work with at my level of spiritual awareness. As I see it, the beauty about this is that as you are able to proceed and grow in spiritual maturity, your increasing spiritual wisdom makes it so that many questions get answered along the way before you need to ask them.

So now, working at my current level of spiritual awareness, after the question, 'Who Am I?', the next most important questions that I need answered in life are: How? What? and Why?

How do I create the What of Why I am here because of Who I Am?

I have always been intrigued by the spiritual school of thought concerning two tenets that relate to how we create, even as I have struggled to really understand them.

The first is that Passion ignites Consciousness and Consciousness ignites Energy which we then use to create. But this passion is not just limited to, or just emanates simply from, your traditional, 'I love cooking; I love making kites and flying them; I love doing jigsaw puzzles.' No; this is a higher form of passion, and the aforementioned activities are our expressions arising from our experiencing this higher form of passion.

The second is that all the answers and everything that a Being needs to create their reality, experience it, learn from it and grow and evolve, are to be found within the Being. One is not to go searching outside of oneself to find the answers and the tools for one's life, and this is particularly true of the energies that one uses to create. We should not keep looking for energy outside of ourselves. The energy is not out there; it is within. And it is all ours to command to serve us because we create it.

So, first of all, what is this higher concept of passion, if it is not quite as straightforward and simple as deciding that you love cooking, so you are going to become a chef? Well, I received the most wonderful answer through my darling sister, Zanubia Zafeera, during one of our marathon three-hour visits on WhatsApp, as she lives in East Sussex, England and I live in Brisbane, Queensland, Australia, and during which we discuss all things spiritual and bring each other up to date on what has been going on in our lives. During our conversation, I found myself once again expressing angst over my lack of understanding of what this higher passion is, and she replied with the following, which for me, demonstrates a deep and beautiful understanding of higher passion – and in the process provides additional clarity about the importance of conscious breathing. She said:

To take the deep breath and "breathe in the energies" is not just a nice idea but a vital key to how we create out of our passion for life!

We are Consciousness- our Consciousness ignites Energy in all its forms to serve us.

Conscious breath ignites Energy - intelligent etheric substance – which becomes imprinted by our conscious passion for what we love. When we breathe in and out whilst at play in our imagination and in deep reflective enjoyment of life - in this moment - we are seeding and growing into manifestation our dreams great and small.

Passion is the pure enjoyment of our life in the moment for its own sake which calls to follow the things we love to do, that bring joy, confidence, capacity – the activity of MASTERY alive in us. Being present to our passion for Life we consciously and organically manifest our Life. We etherically breathe the life we love into being. Baking bread, planting vegetables, singing, doodling, painting, playing an instrument, watching birds, being by the ocean. The "Aaaah and Aha!" – the kinesthetic and sensory awareness of being and feeling ALIVE!

It means we can increasingly and naturally dwell in the sensations, colours and feelings of engaging with what brings out our gifts, skills, the best in us: to create livelihood abundance; to create relationships and partnership abundance – engaging with how we want to interact with others; intimacy, deep communication and feeling. Just two aspects of many forms of abundance we might choose to manifest in our lives.

As I excitedly pondered on all of this, I began to wonder: if Divine creative energy is created within us and not simply floating out there in Creation, waiting for us to grab a-hold of it and make use of it, what is it then that we breathe in when we take the in-breath? How does our passion for life get imprinted on this substance of our in-breath? And what is it that we breathe out, that we then utilize to create?

In answer to these questions, we come back to the profound feeling-thought by Creator Eternal Infinite to know Itself, with the realization that, firstly, it is Its Divine Life Force that we breathe in. And secondly, from Creator Eternal Infinite comes the innate ability by each and every Being to further transform that Divine Life Force.

At the level of the Human Being, our passion for life, expressed as feeling-thoughts, radiate from every particle of our being and imprint and ignite these in-breaths of Divine Life Force, transforming them into forms that we then use to create. I think of the sources of feeling-thoughts – whether from the mental body as thoughts, whether from the emotional body in the form of feelings/emotions, or whether from the spirit body as intuition in its varied forms of manifestation – as like the different but integrated and indispensable components of an engine. The engine only works when all its components are operating and working together. So, no matter the source of the original feeling-thought, the deep rush of feelings of clarity, understanding, excitement, joy and gratitude, at being alive – I exist! – and at loving and appreciating all what we see around us, all combine to ignite the Divine Life Force within, scrambling its countless particles into a myriad frequencies and causing them to flow and bond in myriad ways and transform into something denser than its original form.

It is therefore Divine Life Force, further transformed by human passion, that becomes energy – the energies of Gnost in their innumerable forms of countless frequencies and densities. It is this Divine golden fire of Gnost energies that we use to create our life, our reality.

Gnost means being or possessing the highest Divinely balanced degree, or attributes, or potentials, or form, of or for something – be that the highest Divine purpose, creation or creative expression, manifestation, outcome, solution, experience, perspective (I even received, the highest Divine income!) – that is to the highest Divine benefit of All Concerned. Highest Divine benefit meaning, that which provides the greatest potential for the exercise or demonstration and experience of Divine Living Truths/Principles – eg. truth, joy, justice, beauty, love, freedom with responsibility, compassion, service – all of which lead to the acquisition of Divine wisdom, growth and evolution.

Please excuse the constant reference to Divine . . . Divine . . . Divine, here! I simply greatly desire that the reader understands that it represents the highest purpose of states-of-being, acts, events and experiences, as it is that highest purpose that gives meaning to absolutely everything in Creation.

This therefore means that the Gnost energies always embody all the properties to enable a Being to create and to manifest, the highest Divine expression of anything, or the highest Divine solution to anything; if they so choose, since free will means a Being can choose to use the same energies to manifest otherwise. But when we create with full consciousness of who we truly are, we are able to use our passion, our imagination, our inner knowingness (intuition) and our wisdom to create experiences that are of the highest Divine expression and that are of the highest Divine benefit to all concerned.

And so it is that, indeed, we create Energy and it comes from within us. Thus, with each exhale, we release these energy forms into our auric field, where they become potentials, waiting for us to breathe further life into them to create and manifest our reality. Their ability to immediately go into action to manifest their purpose depends on the intensity of the feeling-thoughts that created them, and with which one continues to feed them. The greater the clarity of purpose and intensity of feeling imbued in the forms, the more developed and defined their properties are, the further they can travel, and the greater are their ability to attract, resonate and bond with similar or complementary energy forms, created and released by oneself or by other Beings. And so it is that you attract into your reality the resources and experiences you require and desire – be they your fellow human beings with whom you can exchange skills, ideas and knowledge; be they ideas and inspiration and the ability to develop and utilize your own gifts; be they financial and other abundances; be they sentiments or feelings that you desire to share and experience; or be they the amazing Divine synchronicities that occur to bring everything together at the right time and in the right circumstances to create your passions, your life experiences, your reality.

Now all you need to do is: to realize that you are a Divine Creator; to realize, therefore, that you create your own reality and are responsible for everything in it and everything that you experience; to realize that you give yourself the experiences you undergo, in order to fully awaken to and expand your awareness of the innate wisdom of the Divine archetypal Truths of Goodness, Beauty and Truth; of Love, Compassion and Service; and of Wisdom, Creative Power and Sovereignty, that are all gifted to you by the indwelling I AM Presence, the God I AM Spark of Love, Life Force and Passion.

A deepening consciousness and acceptance of your own Divinity, coupled with implicit trust in the indwelling I AM Presence and the guidance It provides, enables you to craft amazing adventures that give you the opportunity to acquire ever increasing wisdom through experiencing love, joy, trust, devotion, faith, hope, knowledge, truth, strength, justice, empathy, fairness, compassion, beauty, self-worth, goodness, freedom, responsibility, sovereignty, wisdom, leading by example and leading by serving. You come to have a deeper understanding of the value and the beauty of the Divine Truths – and then finally come to the realization through Enlightenment, that you are Creator God also; that you are God In Action, an expression of God The Creator The **Eternal Infinite** Living Void of Consciousness.

And so it is.

This treatise lays out the foundation for my concept of a New Consciousness Civilization, the details of which follow on from this chapter.

2

Founding Principles of the New Consciousness New Energy Civilization

Based on the spiritual tenets laid out in Chapter 1, the following are the Founding Principles for the New Consciousness New Energy Civilization:

1) That as a Human Expression of Creator God MotherFatherSource, Itself an Expression of Creator Eternal Infinite, you are Creator God also and Co-Creator of Life, Gaia Mother Earth, the Universe and Creation;

2) That life is a journey of awakening to all the Divine wisdom and gifts within you;

3) That, therefore, the purpose of life's journey is the achievement of Enlightenment – **the conscious**

realization that you are Creator God also here on Earth;

4)   That as Creator God also on Earth, you have implicit trust in the **Trinity** that you are – the *Me*, that is your physical Self; *Myself*, that is your Higher Self and the repository of all the wisdom garnered through your life experiences; and I, that is the *I AM Presence*, the God Spark that is the Divinity within every Human Being – and in their loving guidance that you receive;

5)   That as Creator God also on Earth, you have the Divine wisdom and creative power to create and experience a life that is founded upon the Divine Principles of Joy and Truth, Beauty and Goodness, Compassion and Service, Love and Enlightenment, Wisdom and Freedom, Creative Power and Sovereignty;

6)   Therefore, that as an embodied Enlightened Being, you understand and accept that all energies and all states-of-being seek balance. As such, freedom is balanced by responsibility, and the one cannot be separated from the other. Thus, the greater the degree of freedom you enjoy, so to the same degree, the greater the responsibility that you also enjoy;

7)   Therefore, that as an embodied Enlightened Being, you understand and accept that you create your reality and the experiences that you have in life and you accept full responsibility for your life;

8)   Therefore, that as an embodied Enlightened Being, you exemplify and live to the best of your ability a life of ease

and grace, that illuminates the amazing potentials that are there for all Beings, to create for themself a life founded on the Divine Principles, as they also seek their own Enlightenment and enlightened ways to live, thrive, grow and evolve.

3

Constitution for the Lands and Societies of the New Consciousness New Energy Civilization

Therefore, We the People of the New Consciousness New Energy Civilization believe and hold these truths to be self-evident:

RIGHTS:

1)   That all Beings are a Divine Expression of Creator Eternal Infinite and Co-Creators of Life, the Universe and Creation.

2)   Therefore, that all Beings are Co-Creators of Life, Gaia Mother Earth, the Universe and Creation.

3)   Therefore, that all Beings have an inalienable right to exist and thrive here on Gaia Mother Earth.

4)   Therefore, that as Divine Co-creators, all Beings are created equal and are valuable beyond measure.

5)   Therefore, that all Human Beings are created equal and are valuable beyond measure.

6)   Therefore, that All 'Beings' Are of Equal Value.

7)   Therefore, that there is no need to use the artificial medium of money to define the value of anyone or anything.

8)   Therefore, that the use of money and monetary values in society no longer apply and cease to exist in the New Consciousness New Energy Civilization.

9)   Therefore, that all Beings have an inalienable right to enjoy in equal measure the beauty and bounty that Mother Earth offers to all those who dwell on and in Her.

10) Therefore, that the natural state-of-being for all Beings here on Earth is that of abundance, be that in good health, wealth, happiness, knowledge, experience, freedom and wisdom;

11) Therefore, that every Being has the right to exercise, enjoy or benefit from the following freedoms:

a)   freedom to freely but responsibly enjoy and benefit from the beauty and bounty of Earth in all their forms;

b) freedom to directly participate at all levels in the running of their country through the direct process of one-person-one vote referendums;

c) freedom to freely but responsibly speak, write or publish your sentiments;

d) freedom to choose your religious or spiritual beliefs and practices for yourself; **but for yourself only**;

e) in the context of the practise of religious or spiritual beliefs, freedom to peacefully associate and assemble with others who share your religious practices and beliefs, if you so desire;

f) in the context of the practise of religious or spiritual beliefs, freedom to peacefully associate and assemble with others of differing religious and spiritual beliefs and practices for the purposes of practise of the religion or spiritual belief, friendship, acquisition and exchange of ideas, knowledge and understanding;

g) a free press that exercises its freedom with responsibility;

h) trial by jury.

To this list may be added other currently existing legal freedoms that are relevant to the New Consciousness Civilization. These will be reviewed and brought up to date and in line with the current thinking, knowledge, attitudes, realities and aspirations of the New Consciousness

Civilization Communities, as well as all relevant Principles of the New Consciousness New Energy Civilization.

To this list shall also be added other freedoms proposed by the people. The proponents shall explain their proposals, the legal consequences will be spelled out by the judiciary, especially as to how they meet the Principles and legal obligations of the New Consciousness New Energy Civilization and any other internationally accepted legal rulings regarding human rights and the rights of every citizen/Being of the world. The proposals shall then be debated by the public and finally voted on by the people in a referendum.

12) The Founding Principles of the New Consciousness New Energy Civilization, the Constitution for the Lands and Societies of the New Consciousness New Energy Civilization, as well as the two major tenets of All 'Beings' Are of Equal Value, and The Pursuit of Excellence In Service to Self and In Service to All Beings (also referred to as the All 'Beings' Principles in this book) and all their tenets, as stated in this Founding Document, form the foundation and the freedoms of the New Consciousness New Energy Civilization. In order to safeguard this foundation and these freedoms, all Persons have to make themselves fully aware of the following:

a) No Person or Persons may impose or try to impose their religious, spiritual or any other beliefs and practices *on the societies* of the New Consciousness Civilization that in any way seek to violate, deny, restrict, subjugate or eliminate any of the Founding Principles and/or any of the freedoms, rights and responsibilities of the All 'Beings' Principles and/or any of the freedoms, rights and responsibilities of the New Consciousness Civilization Constitution and of all other laws of the land, and their human rights as defined by international laws, whether through peaceful means or through fear, intimidation, aggression, violence or war. The nature and degree of enlightenment of the Societies of the New Consciousness Civilization is such that such acts will not and cannot stand and will not be tolerated.

b) No Person or Persons may impose or try to impose their religious, spiritual or any other beliefs and practices *on another individual or other individuals,* that violates, denies, restricts, subjugates, or eliminates, or in any manner deprives them of any freedoms, rights and responsibilities as stated in the Founding Principles and/or any of the freedoms, rights and responsibilities of the All 'Beings' Principles and/or any of the freedoms, rights and responsibilities of the New Consciousness Civilization Constitution and of all other laws of the land, and their human rights as defined by international laws, whether through peaceful means or through fear, intimidation, aggression, violence or war. The nature and degree of enlightenment of the Societies of the New Consciousness Civilization is such that such acts will not and cannot stand and will not be tolerated.

c) All Persons are prohibited from taking the law into their own hands. Citizens must seek justice through the judicial system, which is readily available and easily accessible no matter the day or the hour.

d) Any and all other tenets that the people of a land deem fit to vote in by referendum that preserve and promote and that do not in any way violate, deny, restrict, subjugate or eliminate any of the freedoms, rights and responsibilities of the Founding Principles and/or any of the freedoms, rights and responsibilities of the All 'Beings' Principles and/or any of the freedoms, rights and responsibilities of the New Consciousness Civilization Constitution and of all other laws of the land, as well as their human rights as defined by international laws.

RESPONSIBILITIES:

1) That all Persons recognize and accept that, as is all of Creation, Gaia Mother Earth is a Living Being as only a Living Being is capable of understanding, nurturing and continuously abundantly catering to the needs of other Living Beings, be they animate or inanimate, who dwell upon and within her;

2) Therefore, that all Persons treat Gaia Mother Earth with the same kindness and respect that is due all 'Beings';

3) Therefore, that all Beings recognize the interdependence of life on Earth and beyond and commit to shouldering their own share of the responsibilities of looking after the Earth and all 'Beings' that thereon and therein dwell or exist;

4) Therefore, that all Persons and all society live their lives and operate on the values of the All 'Beings' Principles,

the Founding Principles and the New Consciousness Civilization Constitution;

5) Therefore, that all Persons and all society understand, accept and undertake practices and abide by all laws that enable all 'Beings' to enjoy great freedom, beauty and abundance that are, at the same time, sustainable and enable the preservation of the beauty and bounty of Gaia Mother Earth for the current generation and for generations to come;

6) Therefore, that the Civil Service (formerly 'government') shall truly be of the people, by the people, for the people, with all decisions pertaining to the conduct of a nation's affairs decided through the vote of the people by referendum;

7) Therefore, that it is the right of all Persons to dissent, disagree and criticize any matter and, especially when done in the public arena, mandatory that it is done with accountability, integrity and honesty and *always* accompanied by proposed reasoned alternatives that can be examined, debated and, if necessary, voted on by the people. Dissent, disagreement and criticism therefore become positive catalysts for negotiation, compromise, change, invention, innovation, growth and evolution;

8) Similarly, therefore, that the citizens of the land are served by a free press in all its forms, but mandatory that the press also serves the citizens of the land with accountability, integrity and honesty, and exercises its freedom with responsibility by basing every story on fact; facts that, if required, must be submitted for and pass

forensic examination and can be upheld as the truth by a court of law. Gossip, whether with or without malicious intent; malicious, uninformed and careless speculation; fabrication and lies will not be tolerated and shall be a violation of the law.

It is important to state here that it should be clear by now that those who desire to experience the joy of living in the New Societies of the New Consciousness New Energy Civilization, as described in this blueprint, shall have attained the level of spiritual maturity and enlightened consciousness that enable them to relate naturally and gracefully to all 'Beings' in a manner that conforms with the ideals of the New Consciousness Civilization, and are willing to continue growing and evolving in order to further their spiritual maturity and deepen their Consciousness. Consequently, some of the tenets stated above and elsewhere in this blueprint, as well as the many rules and regulations that govern society today will either simply not apply, or they will quickly fall by the wayside.

It is also important to reiterate here that sophisticated simplicity is a cornerstone of the New Consciousness New Energy Civilization. Humans should be able to understand and interact with one another, whether in the public or private arena, and understand and interact with the processes, systems and structures of all areas of human endeavour, in an honest and straightforward manner, completely devoid of all the disingenuousness that accompanies so much of human interaction today, that are for the most part born of the relentless pursuit of financial gain.

It would not be far-fetched to state that with the elimination of money and all its systems, structures, rules and regulations, at least fifty percent of all the convoluted rules and regulations that govern our lives today, will disappear.

4

ALL 'BEINGS' ARE OF EQUAL VALUE

There are two elements that form the foundation of the new philosophy for the New Societies of the New Consciousness New Energy Civilization, and for the wellbeing of Mother Earth and all those who dwell in and on her. The first of these is that 'All 'Beings' are of Equal Value'. All 'Beings' meaning:

1)   You and I and all forms of life; everything that exists, i.e., in whatever form **Creator Eternal Infinite** chooses to incarnate on Earth, whether animate or inanimate; and

2)   All forms or manner of choosing to be, of choosing to become, of choosing to manifest through one's creativity, of choosing to experience life. (See Chapter 1 for the full meaning of 'Being')

And 'New Energy' meaning:

1)   The higher vibrating Divine energies that human beings are able to tap into, embody and use, as their consciousness undertakes its journey of expansion towards the quantum leap that is Ascension/ Enlightenment; an expansional creative energy that comes fully into its own at the point when a human being attains their moment of enlightenment – that moment of conscious realization that they are God Also. Adamus Saint-Germain describes the concept in his book, *Live Your Divinity: Inspiration for New Consciousness (Saint-Germain, Adamus; Hoppe, Geoffrey; Hoppe, Linda. Live Your Divinity: Inspirations for New Consciousness. Red Wheel Weiser. Kindle Edition)*; and

2)   New free energy, e.g., cold fusion and other alternative sources of free energy that will soon be discovered, that have already been discovered and that will be revealed, as human consciousness now makes a quantum leap and expands to embrace wonderful new realities.

All 'Beings' Are of Equal Value describes a reality that is based on the premise that all Persons, through the Grace and Power of The Creator are Co-Creators of Life, Gaia, Mother Earth, the Universe and Creation.

As Co-Creators, we understand and accept that All 'Beings', be they animate or inanimate, have their own type of consciousness and have Divine meaning and purpose for incarnating or manifesting on Mother Earth, as all strive individually to become integrated and balanced, to express Divine self through creativity, through experience and the acquisition and expression of knowledge and wisdom, and to evolve.

As Co-Creators, we understand and accept that Gaia, Mother Earth is a Living Being, to be treated with the same kindness and respect that is due all Beings, and that Mother Earth and all 'Beings' in and on her are valuable beyond measure, are therefore invaluable and as such All 'Beings' are of Equal Value.

We understand and accept that abundance, be it in good health, wealth, happiness, knowledge and experience, is the natural state of being for every Being here on Earth; that we all have the right to enjoy the beauty and bounty of Earth equally and freely, whilst at the same time taking responsibility for ensuring maximum utility of all resources taken from the Earth and maximum utility of all systems, structures and products, all of which in one manner or another come from or impact on the Earth and her resources.

As all 'Beings' are of equal value, everybody's work/profession/ societal activity is equal in value to everyone else's. The medical doctor and her/his/their work has exactly the same value as the nurse and his/her/their work, the teacher and his/her/their work, the miner and her/his/their work, the garbage collector and her/his/their work, the physiotherapist and her/his/their work, the electrician and his/her/their work, the astronaut and her/his/their work, the road builder and her/his/their work, the administration officer and his/her/their work, the cleaner and his/her/their work, the airline pilot and her/his/their work, the stay-at-home parent(s) and her/his/their work, the plumber and his/her/their work, the manufacturer and her/his/their work, the head of state and her/his/their work, the civil service workers and their work, etc., etc.

With this understanding comes the realization that there is no longer any need to use the artificial medium of money to give artificial values to anyone and to define most things in society. Therefore, the use of money and monetary values in society no longer applies and cease to exist in the New Consciousness New Energy Civilization.

As all 'Beings' are of equal value and there no longer exists the need to pay anyone or to pay for anything, we now come to realize that we do not need to work to 'earn' a living – to be paid a wage or salary on which we have to manage to live. That whole system ceases to exist. We can now engage in work activities that we have a real passion and aptitude for; that brings us joy and satisfaction.

A SIMPLE EXAMPLE OF HOW THIS WORKS:

A Teacher and a Baker:

1)   The work that a teacher does – who is a teacher because they genuinely love teaching – in teaching adults

or children in a state-of-the-art learning establishment, using their imagination and creativity, as well as state-of-the-art skills, knowledge, methods, equipment, tools and aids, as this is now all possible, is equal in value to the work of a baker – who is a baker because they genuinely love baking – who bakes a delicious variety of food with the freshest ingredients for the public, in a state-of-the-art bakery using their imagination and creativity, as well as state-of-the-art skills, knowledge, methods, equipment, gadgets and aids, as this is now all possible.

2)   Therefore, the teacher is entitled to go to the bakery and take as much bread, cakes and pastries as he/she requires without having to pay for it, and the baker and his children are entitled to attend a learning institution and get taught properly by a teacher without having to pay for it. Just as much as the teacher and her or his family are entitled to reserve air tickets, accommodation and transport, then board an airplane and travel to a destination on holiday without payment in any way, shape or form. Similarly, the baker and his or her family can go out to their favourite restaurant for lunch and then head for the cinema to enjoy a movie (or several) before returning to a lovely home, all with no payment involved.

For those who question how local communities and their environments will be impacted by large numbers of tourists descending upon them now that everyone can travel, regulations that cater to environmental and quality of life sustainability are utilized to control such influxes. For example, countries can impose a quota on the number of tourists that can visit a particular city at any time, to make life manageable and pleasant for those who live in the city and those who desire to visit. (I note in the news that some countries are now beginning to consider something along these lines!)

The quota system will be based on seasons as well as months of the year, to enable the tourism industry to cater to people's wishes as much as possible. So, tourists can still choose when they wish to visit a place and their wishes will be matched as closely as possible. As visitors depart, so there become vacancies in the quota for tourists in the queue to fill. The quota will also allow for casual visitors from within the same country who, for instance, use their own private transport to visit the city, who have relatives in the city and so do not stay in a hotel, or who are business or professional people who regularly or irregularly visit the city for varying lengths of stay.

The quota system is a fully computerized system that is integrated into the airline, hotel, tourism and any other relevant industry systems, country-wide and world-wide. I believe that the technology already exists to enable nations to put such a system in place, or for such a system to be developed and employed with little delay. With such a system in place, cities/communities are now also able to carry out major renovation works to upgrade their amenities and facilities to state-of-the-art standards, which may result in increased tourist-handling capacity without breaching their environmental and quality of life sustainability regulations.

5

THE PURSUIT OF EXCELLENCE IN SERVICE TO SELF AND IN SERVICE TO ALL BEINGS

The second element of the new philosophy is that, as 'All 'Beings' are of Equal Value' and therefore money and all its related systems, institutions and values cease to exist, the current unrelenting pursuit of profit and all the other money-based values that underpin human civilization and motivate human society today, are replaced by a new Standard – *The Pursuit of Excellence In Service to Self and In Service to All Beings.*

This new approach to life and to living brings about a tremendous change in people's lives. It creates a tremendous increase in the mental, emotional and physical wellbeing of the populace and in their morale and enthusiasm; and because people can now engage in work that they genuinely like to do, as opposed to working in order to earn a living, they are highly motivated.

This leads to a tremendous birth in creativity and problem solving. People now take a lot of pride in what they do and desire to do it in the best, most efficient, most effective, most humane, most beneficial and most Earth-friendly way possible and they set out to find ways to accomplish this. This leads to new attitudes and approaches to doing things. It leads to the invention of new tools, processes, systems and structures and as a result the way we live changes completely – and a New Consciousness New Energy Civilization is born!

6

RESPONSIBILITIES OF THE CITIZENS OF THE NEW SOCIETIES OF THE NEW CONSCIOUSNESS CIVILIZATION

In this New Consciousness Civilization, every Human Being comes to recognize the interdependence of life on Earth and commit to shouldering their own share of the responsibility of looking after the Earth and all 'Beings' that thereon and therein dwell or exist. As such, there will be things that we collectively or as individuals can own, but with ownership comes responsibilities that owners have to commit to; and there will be things that we collectively or as individuals cannot own, but for which we are still collectively or individually responsible for looking after. The latter are things from which Human and all other Beings are meant to take only what they need when they need it, or share, for they are the finite and infinite resources of Earth, gifted to All 'Beings' and therefore beyond ownership by any individual or groups of individual Human Beings.

Thus, the citizens of the New Consciousness Civilization are an educated citizenry that understand and accept the responsibilities of creating and running their own lives with honesty and with integrity, and they accept the responsibilities of fashioning and running their countries on all levels with a hands-on approach, with honesty and with integrity.

Consequently, politics and politicians cease to exist. The laws of the land require that every man, woman and child acquire an education to enable them to eventually engage in an 'Activity Beneficial to Society and to Self' (as described in Chapter 9), and it requires that every woman, man and youth educate themself about local community, national and international issues. It is the responsibility of every citizen to know and understand the issues, so that they are able to make informed decisions about the matters that affect their lives on all levels, as, through state-of-the-art technology, every citizen has to vote regularly in referendums on laws, regulations, policies, processes, systems, structures and undertakings in all areas of human endeavour that make up the realities of life.

By doing so, the citizens of a country are able to inform, instruct and guide their Civil Service – a Civil Service that is there solely to serve the people (as described in Chapters 24 & 27).

And so it is, that true democracy returns to the people. It is one person—one vote and governing a country is truly by the people, of the people, for the people.

7

SOPHISTICATED SIMPLICITY

A major thrust of the New Consciousness New Energy Civilization is to bring a sophisticated simplicity to human life. However, simplicity does not mean primitivity.

It means making life uncomplicated – simple, easy to understand things, easy to take comprehensive action on things; straightforward – no padding, no deviousness, no cheating and lying in order to steal; streamlined – everything is seamless in operation and yet sophisticated. Life is lived with ease and grace.

It means eliminating, or reducing to an absolute minimum, red tape, bureaucracy and dishonesty as are to be found in government today; eliminating the even more dishonest and devious practices to be found in business and industry today; totally eliminating the dishonest and useless spin as is found in the advertising industry today; and the even more useless chatter, and perverted, manipulative and destructive speculation and lies, as are found in the media today.

It is placing honesty, responsibility, integrity, self-respect and mutual respect among the bedrocks of the New Consciousness New Energy Civilization. All institutions will be based upon, reflect and promote this simplicity. The Civil Service in particular – which will be of the people, by the people and for the people and whose raison d'etre is purely to serve all Beings – has to operate within these principles, thereby helping to set the tone for society.

In every step of the way, the interface, and in particular the technological interface between processes, systems, structures and human beings will be straightforward and uncomplicated, even though the results of interactions are very comprehensive and sophisticated and the inner workings of some of the processes, systems and structures are necessarily quite complex.

It will be mandatory that all public service, Civil Service and in particular legal communication be in plain language, uncomplicated and with minimal or no use of professional jargon.

The farcical levels of complexity of many aspects of human endeavour today, especially in the world of finance, and the equally farcical levels of red tape and sheer waste to be found in government and industry today, cease to exist.

8

QUALITY, QUANTITY AND UTILITY

In the New Consciousness Civilization, quality, i.e., degree of excellence, fitness for use and the ability to satisfy needs and desires, is of paramount importance – quality of life, quality of the environment, quality of products, quality of services – and it is by what all things are measured first and foremost.

In the New Consciousness Civilization where money and all its structures no longer exist, the effect of products, services, processes, systems, structures, regulations and laws, on the environment and on the wellbeing of all 'Beings', as well as their degree of usefulness and degree of excellence in service to all 'Beings, are what now replace cost. The questions we ask are (how much in the questions below refer to degree/to what extent and **not to cost**):

1) how and by how much (degree) do these elements increase ease of operations?

2) how and by how much do these elements increase the efficient use of resources – i.e., increased number of end products, maintaining the same or attaining increased quality, but using the same or less quantity of resources?

3) how and by how much do these elements increase the quality of end products?

4) how and by how much do these elements improve upon the requirements of environmental standards and regulations?

5) Answers to the first 4 questions above go towards answering this 5th question, which is: how and by how much do these elements improve the quality of life of all Beings?

Therefore, the utility of products, services, processes, systems, structures, regulations and laws and to what degree they improve the quality of life are what determine their value to life, their usefulness to life, their reason for being.

Each one of us will be expected to provide quality service and products for our fellow citizens and to expect the same in return, creating a society that strives for excellence in service to self and in service to all Beings.

9

ACTIVITY BENEFICIAL TO SOCIETY AND TO SELF

To ensure that the Earth, the environment, life and society thrive, run smoothly and that the needs of every 'Being' are met, all persons of sound mind and body, who are not babies or children below school age, have by law to engage in an Activity Beneficial to Society and to Self (**ABSAS or Activity**), that brings an immediate or eventual benefit to society and to themselves. They therefore have to engage in exercising a profession or service that brings a benefit to society and to themselves; or they have to be attending an educational institution and acquiring knowledge and skills that will enable them to engage in, or enhance their performance of, an Activity that brings benefit to society and to themselves.

This requirement is similar to what transpires in the world today, but with the following major differences:

As everybody's work/profession/societal activity is equal in value to everyone else's and money and all its related systems, structures and values no longer exist, the need to earn a living in order to obtain the money or means by which to live no longer exists. This frees up every human being to engage in the pursuit of excellence in service to self and in service to all Beings and to select an *Activity Beneficial to Society and to Self* for which they have – and *must* have – a genuine passion and aptitude, i.e., ability, natural bent, a natural interest, skill(s), talent, gift, capacity, fitness, propensity. Indeed, these qualities will be mandatory prerequisites when determining career paths and goals and education and training requirements. Determining these will be a formal process in which every individual will have a trained counsellor to assist them in making these choices.

We cannot fail to understand why we are to give of our best to provide and maintain goods and services at the highest standard for our own use and the use of others when we are undertaking an Activity that:

1)   we have real joy in doing and therefore find it energizing, pleasurable and that does not feel like work;

2)   we have, or can acquire and can continuously improve upon, the skills required to do the Activity to the highest standard;

3)   we carry out our Activity in an environment that is state-of-the-art because we are equipped with the best equipment and tools; we operate in the safest and most comfortable working environment to do the Activity and we have first-class support structures in our place of Activity;

4)   we are able to concentrate fully on our Activity because we are not distracted with worry about how to pay bills, meet life's necessities and desires, or obtain assistance;

5)   we leave our place of Activity and return to state-of-the-art dwellings in superb environments and communities with state-of-the-art amenities and first-class support structures.

Under the New Consciousness Civilization, the week will consist of the following:

1)   Three (3) days of full engagement with one's Activity;

2)   A two (2)-day weekend for family togetherness, leisure activities and rest; and

3)   Two (2) Personal Days. Everyone will be encouraged to set aside these 2 days as:

a)   a person's time to concentrate on pampering themselves and meeting their needs as individuals, such as pursuing spiritual enlightenment, self-development, health, recreational and sports activities;

b)   the time for community engagement activities, i.e:

(i)   attending community and national seminars, workshops and meetings on local, national and international issues;

(ii)   submitting proposals to the Civil Service;

(iii)   voting in referendums on issues;

(iv)   participating in other community engagement activities (e.g., you are a member of a glee club and the club has agreed to put on a show at a children's hospital).

Areas of Activity that need to run 24/7 will be covered by shift work that will enable shift workers to still meet all the requirements stated above.

4)   Activities beneficial to society and to self encompass all areas of human endeavour, whether it is serving society as a doctor, nurse, teacher, furniture maker, as a homemaker raising children, a public servant, a visual artist, a professional sports person, a performing artist, a student, or someone engaged in the many new professions and areas of service that will arise due to the advent of the New Consciousness Civilization.

5)   A person can engage in as many Activities as they like but they cannot live their lives without being engaged in any Activity, unless they are retired and choose to do so. Every person of sound body and mind and below the retirement age must engage in at least one Activity that is beneficial to society and to self.

6)   To prevent people putting up storefronts as Activities and then doing little or nothing at all, all Activities have to meet certain criteria in order to be considered legitimate and the policies governing this matter must, as a minimum, enable the following:

a) every person's Activity or Activities, whether that is a business, a profession, home duties or attending an institution of learning, will be registered and monitored by the Department for ABSAS Monitoring and Assistance and/or the Department of Education, Activities and Training and the information will be available to the public on the National Governance Website;

b) all Activities have to meet the performance targets set for their particular kind of Activity, i.e. a certain amount of turnover, or a certain number of clients, or some other prescribed degree of activity on a regular basis, all of which are determined by the type of Activity; e.g., the baker has to have a turnover of, for example, 100 items of baked goods per day; a learning institution has to cater to no less than a certain number of students per year and has to demonstrate that it is successful in its undertaking based on the standards that the students attain each year; a physiotherapist has to cater to the needs of a certain number of clients per month and has to have a certain number of successfully concluded cases per year, etc, etc. These figures will always be in the form of a range and averaged for the whole year to allow for seasonal changes, good periods and not so good periods, good days and not so good days. Stock turnover, client numbers, quality of service and the benefit that an Activity brings to the local community are the four important factors that determine whether an Activity is legitimate or not;

c) therefore, Stock-taking through a nation-wide state-of-the-art system becomes a vital tool in ascertaining the legitimacy of Activities, and meeting performance targets and the tracking of these and other elements of an Activity become major undertakings for all Activities;

d) all business Activity owners are advised to review their businesses on a regular basis, and by law once every two years, in order to:

    (i)   assess their legitimacy and take any steps required to maintain or improve legitimacy;

    (ii)   undertake repairs and renovations to maintain workplace health and safety and any other relevant standards, as well as bring their business into alignment with new technologies, processes and updated regulations.

e) on a quarterly basis all business Activities have to submit a report electronically to the Department for ABASA Monitoring and Assistance for analysis to ensure that Activities are legitimate by meeting performance targets;

f) those consistently failing to meet the performance targets for their Activity within a prescribed period will automatically be advised to seek the services of a business expert/ advisor/ mentor to assist them in establishing a legitimate Activity. The aim of this undertaking is not to witch-hunt, harass, penalize and instill fear in people, but rather to ensure a strong focus on helping people to run legitimate and viable Activities for which they have a genuine passion and to ensure that the infrastructure is in place to provide the additional support that Activities and Activity owners require;

g) to increase client base and make an Activity legitimate, an owner can easily obtain the services of an expert to advise and assist them in doing so. Among the options an owner has are for example the following:

(i) expand range of products;

(ii) expand range of services;

(iii) combine products with services;

(iv) specialize – products, services and hours of operation;

(v) add an additional complimentary Activity or Activities as new start-up(s) or by merging or partnering with another/others who are also looking to merge or partner, to expand their client base to make their Activity viable;

(vi)   relocate;

(vii) change Activity altogether;

(viii) close down your under-performing business Activity and offer your services/skills to the owner of another business Activity.

HOW THIS CAN WORK:

Today, *Stocktaking and Point of Sale* technology are quite sophisticated and continue to advance in their sophistication. What exists already today can be easily adapted to fit the requirements of the New Consciousness Civilization.

Thus, experts in the field of stocktaking/point of sale technology will be called upon to put in place a state-of-the-art National Stocktaking System that at minimum will achieve the following objectives:

1)   As is currently the case, all components of goods and services, as well as the manufacturers of the goods and suppliers of services, are assigned a barcode to facilitate stock-taking and as is currently the case, these barcodes contain as much information about a product and its manufacturer as is possible;

2) Every Activity providing goods and services to customers must be connected to the nation-wide check-in and check-out stock-taking system, with the check-in

stock-taking facility situated in a designated delivery and receiving bay. Here the details of all supplies received by a business are inserted into the system;

3) The check-out stock-taking facility will be situated at the customer pick-up or despatch point, which as is the case today will normally be a shop with check-out bays;

4) To ensure that suppliers are indeed providing goods and services to the public, each and every person, as is the case today with bank cards, will have a Personal Acquisition Card (PAC), or some sort of unique personal identification marker that they, as customers, have to insert in the system at the check-out point and against which all goods and services they acquire are recorded. If the customer runs a business Activity, they must also have a Business Activity Acquisition Card (BAAC) for each business, that is swiped at every check-out point and against which all goods and services they acquire for the business are recorded;

5) The checkout point at a business Activity no longer counts cash but instead becomes a check-out stock-taking facility. Details of goods or products supplied or utilized in the provision of a service that are swiped at the check-out point must match the details put into the system during the check-in stock-taking process. At this point the system also generates other information such as PAC or BAAC details, the check-out date of a product, how much of a product has been checked-out to customers and how much is still in stock, etc, etc;

6) To ensure the veracity of the barcode system's data and that turnover is being accurately measured:

a) When a product passes through the check-out point and is recognized as a product supplied by that business Activity because the details at the check-out point match the details in the system inserted during the check-in process, a verification code is assigned to that specific supply in the system. If necessary, the verification code is also stamped onto a label that is affixed to the packaging of that specific supply;

b) It will be a legal requirement that all items packaged together in a carton are properly individually labelled and coded and must match the label and codes on the carton. The system will verify these details when the carton of products is picked up by a customer. If the items from the carton are sold individually, the system will be able to match and link the individual items to the details for the carton at the check-out point;

c) In the case where goods are bought in bulk and then re-packaged in smaller quantities by the business owner for supply to the public, the details for the bulk product must first be entered into the system. The details on the labels printed out by the system for the re-packaged goods must link back to the details of the bulk product as it was originally checked into the system, and also contain new details such as the weight of the product in its new packaging, date when repackaged and by which business Activity, etc, etc;

d) today technology makes it possible for customers to help themselves to products that are loose and sold in bulk, eg. meats, vegetables, fruits, nuts, etc, insert them into packaging, weigh the package on a scale placed right next to the product and that automatically prints out a barcode label with relevant details, which the customer then affixes to the package. The barcode is then scanned at the check-out register.

e) once a product has passed through the checkout point, it cannot simply be put back on the shelf if returned. Doing so will set of an alarm system that will cause checkout points to grind to a halt. The returned or exchanged product has to be swiped back into the store at the check-in point, as per the process in the system designed to take care of returned items;

f) spoiled or damaged and therefore unusable goods will be entered as such in the system and disposed of in the proper manner.

The above is a simple description just to give an initial idea of what is required as part of the infrastructure of the New Consciousness Civilization. As stated earlier, the Civil Service will work hand-in-hand with experts in this field to create, install, maintain and upgrade a nationwide system that meets at all times the standards of excellence and sophisticated simplicity required.

7) Provided all possible safeguards can be put in place to ensure this cannot be abused, the Civil Service could also consider implementing the following: To assist members of

the public, especially those of under-performing business Activities who have been advised to seek help, to locate skilled technicians, experts, advisors and mentors, the Civil Service could perhaps consider establishing and maintaining a National Governance Business Activity Assistance Register – an extensive database on which Activity owners may register themselves as being available for work in the private sector or as experts to advise and work with others in the private sector, once they meet the standards required for such registration. Registrants may be asked to sit exams to demonstrate their competence; especially their knowledge of any recently updated policies and regulations that govern their profession. This registration is for work on private projects and contracts being conducted by members of the public and is not for civil works for which the award of contracts must be by tender. To avoid the system descending into chaos, the following will apply:

a) The whole system will be highly computerized. And so, as an example: successful applicants will be registered on the computerized nation-wide/state-wide/local database, streamed according to Activity and automatically queued within their designated stream. As the Civil Service Departments receive requests to provide the name and contact details of an expert or advisor or mentor, these are fed into the database, which automatically supplies the details of the first expert/advisor/mentor in the queue of the relevant stream. As soon as an expert, advisor or mentor indicates that they have a contract for a stated period –

the recipient of their service has to also confirm this – their name and details are taken off the list and 'parked' in the system for the stated period. As soon as a contract is completed to a client's satisfaction – and this has to be attested to by the client – their details are 'un-parked' and go to the back of the queue of their stream.

b) This whole system is highly computerized, and individuals cannot alter the queue or choose the expert or advisor for an initial contract. However, both parties to a contract can mutually agree to extend a contract in order to finish a project, or to commence a different stage of the same project. Should a business Activity owner and an expert/advisor/mentor find that they are unable to work together, their contract can be mutually immediately terminated, and a new request submitted by the business Activity owner. Such requests take priority over brand new business Activities and are automatically immediately dealt with to prevent a business Activity with major works in progress from being delayed and destroyed. The system automatically parks, un-parks, archives and deletes registrants' details. As the request for an expert or advisor and the submission and verification of a contract are all done online, this is a process that can be done from a person's home.

c) At regular intervals, those wishing to remain on the database have to sit exams in one form or another to demonstrate that they are keeping abreast of new developments and any new regulations in their profession. This is important for two reasons:

(i)   it is of paramount importance that those offering their services as an expert, adviser or mentor, can offer a service of excellence to their clients

(ii)   in many cases, those offering their services under this program can claim this as their ABSAS, if they meet all the other criteria to do so. Regular testing ensures that service providers who make such a claim, continue to meet the requirement that they provide a service of excellence to their clients. It also identifies those who need additional support in maintaining their standard of excellence, so that the support can be provided

d) Every year those on the database are required to confirm or update their contact details and indicate if they wish to continue to be registered on the database or not and to delete or archive their details themselves from the database if so desired. If no update response activity is detected online within the prescribed period in relation to an entry on the database, the entry is automatically archived. Details are finally deleted in accordance with record-keeping regulations.

8)   It will be the law that all business Activity owners run an apprenticeship program for those who learning on the job better suits their temperament and aptitudes, with the number of apprentices dependent on the size of the

business Activity. These apprenticeships will no longer be the hit-or-miss, half-baked and blatantly exploitative affair that too many apprenticeships are today, since both the business Activity and the teaching institution can now have all the skilled manpower and resources required to properly tutor, monitor and mentor the apprentices in every program to the highest standards possible. This now also provides interesting Activities to benefit society and self for people who have a passion for teaching.

9) Similarly and by law, all business Activity owners, in collaboration with the teaching institutions, have to provide to the highest standard possible the tutoring, monitoring and mentoring of students undertaking the *'Practicals'* or *'Work Placement'* component of any relevant course of study from any institution, as Activity owners now have the skilled manpower and abundant resources to do so.

10

PARENTING IN THE NEW CONSCIOUSNESS CIVILIZATION

The Rules:

0 – 1 years: 2 parents stay at home fulltime for 1 year

1 – 4 years: 1 parent stays at home fulltime for 3 years to facilitate the raising of the child; 1 parent has to engage in part-time Activity. Parents may take turns in staying at home, according to flexible arrangements worked out by all parties concerned.

5 – 7 years: 2 parents have to engage in part-time Activity, in addition to the Activity of raising the child/children.

8 years: Raising a child is no longer recognized as a fulltime Activity once a child turns 8 years of age. Both parents have to return to fulltime Activity.

Retirement: A possibility is that the retirement age is such as to balance with the number of the young entering the Activity phase. This may mean that the retirement age changes from year to year, or a fixed interval, eg. every 3 years.

A SIMPLE EXAMPLE OF HOW THIS WORKS:

Year of Birth	Date After 12 Mths	John	Susan	Jack	Mary	Parents: Dan & Danielle
1/1/60	1/1/61	0 -1 yrs				Dan & Danielle stay home to look after newborn John
1/2/61	1/1/62	1-2 yrs				Danielle stays home to look after John; Dan engages in a part-time Activity. Parents may take turns staying at home according to a flexible arrangement agreed by all parties involved
1/2/62	1/1/63	2 - 3 yrs	0 - 1 yrs			Dan & Danielle stay home to look after John and newborn Susan
1/2/63	1/1/64	3 - 4 yrs	1 - 2 yrs			Danielle stays home to look after John and Susan; Dan engages in a part-time Activity. Parents may take turns staying at home according to a flexible arrangement agreed by all parties involved
1/2/64	1/1/65	4 - 5 yrs.	2 - 3 yrs	0 - 1 yrs		Dan & Danielle stay home to look after John, Susan and newborn Jack
1/2/65	1/1/66	5 - 6 yrs	3 - 4 yrs	1 - 2 yrs		Danielle stays at home to look after John, Susan and Jack; Dan engages in a part-time Activity. Parents may take turns staying at home according to a flexible arrangement agreed by all parties involved

Year of Birth	Date After 12 Mths	John	Susan	Jack	Mary	
1/2/66	1/1/67	6 – 7 yrs	4 – 5 yrs	2 – 3 yrs	0 – 1 yrs	Dan & Danielle stay home to look after John, Susan, Jack and newborn Mary
1/2/67	1/1/68	7 - 8 yrs	5 - 6 yrs	3 - 4 yrs	1 – 2 yrs	Danielle stays at home to look after John, Susan, Jack and Mary; Dan engages in a part-time Activity. Parents may take turns staying at home according to a flexible arrangement agreed by all parties involved
1/2/68	1/1/69	8 - 9 yrs	6 - 7 yrs	4 - 5 yrs	2 - 3 yrs	Danielle stays at home to look after Susan, Jack and Mary (John); Dan engages in a part-time Activity. Parents may take turns staying at home according to a flexible arrangement agreed by all parties involved
1/2/69	1/1/70	9 - 10 yrs	7 - 8 yrs	5 - 6 yrs	3 - 4 yrs	Danielle stays at home to look after Susan, Jack and Mary (John); Dan engages in a part-time Activity. Parents may take turns staying at home according to a flexible arrangement agreed by all parties involved

PARENTING LEAVE GUIDE

The following is given as a guide, based on the example on the previous page.

Parents are entitled to a minimum of 4 years to a maximum of 14 years parenting leave on the parenting schedule.

FOR ONE (1) CHILD

One (1) parent stays home for 4 years fulltime + 4 years part-time = 8 years.

One (1) parent stays home for 1 year fulltime + 7 years part-time = 8 years.

Therefore, parents with one (1) child may stay away from fulltime Activity for a maximum of 8 years after which they have to return to fulltime Activity.

Parents may take turns in staying at home according to flexible arrangements worked out by all parties concerned.

FOR TWO (2) CHILDREN WITH A GAP OF TWO (2) YEARS BETWEEN THE FIRST AND SECOND CHILD

One (1) parent stays home for 7 years fulltime + 3 years part-time = 10 years.

One (1) parent stays home for 2 year fulltime + 8 years part-time = 10 years.

Therefore, parents with two (2) children may stay away from fulltime Activity for a maximum of 10 years after which they have to return to fulltime Activity.

Parents have to return to maximum Activity during periods that exceed the maximum parenting leave period between the birthing of one child and the next.

Parents may take turns in staying at home according to flexible arrangements worked out by all parties concerned.

FOR THREE (3) CHILDREN WITH A GAP OF TWO (2) YEARS BETWEEN THE SECOND AND THIRD CHILD

One (1) parent stays home for 9 years fulltime + 3 years part-time = 12 years.

One (1) parent stays home for 3 year fulltime + 9 years part-time = 12 years.

Therefore, parents with three (3) children may stay away from fulltime Activity for a maximum of 12 years after which they have to return to fulltime Activity.

Parents have to return to maximum Activity during periods that exceed the maximum parenting leave period between the birthing of one child and the next.

Parents may take turns in staying at home according to flexible arrangements worked out by all parties concerned.

FOR FOUR (4) CHILDREN WITH A GAP OF TWO (2) YEARS BETWEEN THE THIRD AND FOURTH CHILD

One (1) parent stays home for 11 years fulltime + 3 years part-time = 14 years.

One (1) parent stays home for 4 year fulltime + 10 years part-time = 14 years.

Therefore, parents with four (4) children may stay away from fulltime Activity for a maximum of 14 years, after which they have to return to fulltime Activity.

Parents have to return to maximum Activity during periods that exceed the maximum parenting leave period between the birthing of one child and the next.

Parents may take turns in staying at home according to flexible arrangements worked out by all parties concerned.

FOR FIVE (5) CHILDREN AND OVER

The maximum parenting leave period of 14 years cannot be exceeded even if parents have more than four children.

However, both parents are entitled to six (6) months fulltime parenting leave at the birth of a fifth and each subsequent child.

On completion of six (6) months parenting leave, both parents have to return to fulltime Activity.

1) As is the case today, it will be compulsory that all children first have to acquire a basic education and then acquire further education, that will enable them to later as adults engage in an Activity beneficial to society and themselves.

2) Raising children by parents or caretakers is fully recognized as a legitimate Activity and would operate according to a process such as the following:

a) For quality of life and environmental sustainability reasons, people will be encouraged to, or it will be the law that people, have no more than 4 children. It is highly likely, however, that with the freedoms and opportunities that societies of the New Consciousness Civilization will enjoy, a natural birth control process will occur as people pace events in their lives to enable everyone in the family to accomplish as many things as possible in their lifetime and also enjoy quality of life. Suffice it to say that this issue will be thoroughly discussed, debated and decided upon by the citizens of the land through a referendum;

b) For the first year of a child's life (0 – 1 yr old), both parents are entitled to stay at home and raise that child. During their year-long absence, Business owners can make their own private arrangements with someone, or obtain the services of a qualified person through the National Governance Business Activity Assistance Register, to manage their business Activity;

c) From 1 – 5 years of age, one parent is entitled to stay at home to facilitate the raising of that child, whilst the other parent engages in an Activity on a part time basis. Parents may take turns in staying at home according to a flexible arrangement of their own choosing;

d) From 6 – 7 years of age, both parents have to return to a part-time Activity in addition to the Activity of raising the child. For example, one parent could engage in an Activity during the morning hours whilst the second parent looks after the child at that time. Both parents then switch places in the afternoon; or both parents could work for half a day, whilst their child goes to school, and then spend the rest of the day with their child. Once again parents may put in place a flexible arrangement of their own choosing;

e) On a child turning 8 years of age, raising a child is no longer recognized as a full time Activity and parents have to devote normal full-time hours to an Activity.

These ages here are merely indicative. Top experts in the field dealing with the nurturing of children in all its aspects and who have good innovative ideas will be assigned the task of developing this policy in consultation with the public. The age range of the various stages cannot be extended arbitrarily, once they have been agreed upon, but parents will have the flexibility to shorten the periods if they so desire, based on the capabilities of their child and with the formal approval of a certified childcare expert. The policy will have specific regulations for children who require special care due to an inability. The policy has to be approved by the public through a referendum.

11

DEPARTMENT FOR ABSAS MONITORING AND ASSISTANCE

A Department for ABSAS Monitoring and Assistance is set up to monitor the performance of:

1)   all industrial, manufacturing and exchange business Activities; and

2)   all professional services business Activities

that are registered as an Activity Beneficial to Society and to Self. It also has full access to the National Education and Training Database created and maintained by the Department of Education, Activities and Training, if and when it requires information on the ABSAS of everyone else in the country.

Working closely with all the other Departments of the Civil Service, and with scientists and experts in all areas of the business sector, the Department for ABSAS Monitoring and Assistance, is responsible for:

1)   creating and maintaining a master *National ABSAS Database*. The Department receives up-to-the-minute data from all the other Departments of the Civil Service and any other relevant bodies, that enables it to track and analyze the movement of all goods and services, so as to be able to provide information of the highest standard that will enable business Activities to stay legitimate and pursue excellence in their provision of goods and services to their customers and clients. The public accesses this information through the National Governance ABSAS Database on the National Governance interactive website;

2)   to that end, the creation, maintenance, expansion and upgrade of the *National Stocktaking System* falls under the jurisdiction of this Department and it is the foundation for the National ABSAS Database;

3)   creating and maintaining a master *National Business Activity Assistance Register*, by obtaining, collating and inputting relevant data from members of the public who apply, and/or checking data inserted by applicants directly into the system through the National Governance website portal, so that the Register can act as an accurate and comprehensive resource for business Activity owners seeking expert advice and mentoring to build legitimate Activities. The public accesses this information through the

National Governance Business Activity Assistance Register on the National Governance interactive website;

4) reviewing and overhauling the practice of *Planned Obsolescence* and putting in place a revised system that serves to eliminate over-production and waste, in keeping with the objectives of the New Consciousness Civilization. To that end, and working with all aforementioned expertise, the Department will:

a) in accordance with the revised system, determine the specific products that must have a Minimum-Use period (as described in Chapter 17);

b) in accordance with the revised system, determine accurate Use-By and Minimum-Use periods and set out the regulations and procedures about how these are determined and applied;

c) oversee the manufacture and distribution of the instruments of application of ABSAS systems and fulfil whatever responsibilities the Department has to put in place the systems, tools and processes to ensure that every product has a Use-By date at point of manufacture and/or a Minimum-Use period at point of acquisition that commences on the date of acquisition;

d) work very closely with the relevant Civil Service Departments and the public to ensure that the system works properly and efficiently in all of its aspects: regulations; procedures; manufacture and distribution of instruments of application; implementation of the system; maintenance of the system and the instruments of application; research and development of the system for continuous quality and systems improvement.

12

TECHNOLOGY AND EDUCATION

Technology and an educated public are indispensable pillars of the foundation upon which the New Consciousness New Energy Civilization is built and are crucial to its success – success in its implementation, success in its maintenance and success in its evolution. Thus, the importance of honouring the human imagination and its capacity to create, as well as the knowledge and wisdom that come from an *inner knowing*, from one's intuition, can never be over-stated or over-estimated, as they are the source and the food for human creativity and invention and innovation of the kind of education, science and technology required for the establishment, maintenance and evolution of the New Consciousness Civilization.

Consequently, matters of the greatest urgency and priority in the New Consciousness Civilization are:

1) Finding alternatives to Earth's finite resources, in particular oil and its by-product – energy. In this regard, it is important that scientists and visionaries who have a deep connection to the Earth and an understanding of the New Consciousness New Energy Civilization and the need for it, turn their full attention to the research and development of alternatives such as cold fusion and static energy (is there a relationship between the two?) as new source(s) of clean, abundant and free energy for mankind.

Once again, as Adamus Saint-Germain explains in his book, *Live Your Divinity: Inspiration for New Consciousness (Saint-Germain, Adamus; Hoppe, Geoffrey; Hoppe, Linda. Live Your Divinity: Inspirations for New Consciousness. Red Wheel Weiser. Kindle Edition)*, the ability of humanity to discover free energy, such as cold fusion, and be able to use it to serve humankind peacefully, results from the increasing enlightenment of human consciousness; results from a higher consciousness that has matured enough to connect with and utilize the higher vibrating Divine energies of Creation. I believe it would be safe to say that this is not something that many scientists may be aware of or would even choose to accept and it lies outside the environment that enables them to use their usual methods to prove that something exists.

Those brave scientists struggling to make this a reality, now have to think and act way outside the box, recognize that their work is as much a spiritual journey as it is a scientific one, and focus on Divine Consciousness in their research.

2) In the New Consciousness New Energy Civilization, therefore, scientists, visionaries, futurists and spiritualists all work together in a new kind of science to find alternatives and make incredible new discoveries. I believe that the bravest of the brave in the scientific community now have an opportunity to pioneer this fantastic new field of science based on an understanding of Divine Consciousness. And, with scientists and visionaries no longer constrained by financial considerations, research, invention, development and innovation will be the fastest growing and evolving fields of human endeavour.

3) The creation and establishment of the technological infrastructure for the New Consciousness Civilization, including electronic voting. There exists already in the world today

technology that can be used, either as is or with varying degrees of modification, to establish the foundations of the New Consciousness Civilization.

4) As stated in Chapter 7, ensuring that the technological interface between processes, systems, structures and human beings is straightforward and uncomplicated, even though the results of interactions are very comprehensive and sophisticated and the inner workings of many of the processes, systems and structures are necessarily quite complex.

5) Technology makes many things possible and simplifies, streamlines and brings consistency to structures, systems and processes, resulting in greater speed, efficiency and accuracy. It assists in maintaining impartiality, equality and privacy and it contributes greatly to the fun, excitement, elegance and ease of life.

All this is true of technology, only when it is used to serve humanity, and not used to subjugate humanity to serving it.

6) As in the New Consciousness New Energy Civilization scientists and visionaries are no longer constrained by the need to secure funds for research, enable their financial backers to make a profit and satisfy shareholders, scientists can devote their time and energies to their true calling of being pioneers,

happy, willing and able to go against all conventional beliefs and chase down every non-conforming, unexpected, bizarre and baffling result, condition or anomaly and find that they are in fact signals beckoning humanity to step through doorways to wonderful new discoveries and realities.

7) If this practice does not already exist, on graduation from their course of study, every scientist, indeed every graduate of an educational institution, shall take an oath to be a true pioneer. This oath shall be renewed, for example, every 3 years at a ceremony held by their alma mater, where the pioneering works achieved by any of its attendees or graduates are announced and, where possible, put on display. Such recognition by peers and by the general public acts as a great source of pride, inspiration and motivation for the individuals concerned and for all others.

8) Part of the oath that every graduate – and every member of the Civil Service – will take is that technology, systems, structures, processes, laws, rules and regulations are all totally meaningless without Humans and other Beings. These tools of service and support are therefore created purely to serve and support the Human and other Beings that dwell on and in the Earth. Therefore, these tools of service and support have to be comprehensive and flexible in order to serve every individual with excellence and they

cannot be used to discriminate against, devalue, subordinate or enslave any Human or other Being on Earth.

9) At every opportunity and through every means possible, the citizens of the New Communities of the New Consciousness New Energy Civilization must be made aware and reminded that they are in charge – in charge of themselves, in charge of their communities, in charge of their countries and ultimately in charge of the world. They must therefore constantly strive to exercise the freedoms and responsibilities that this reality brings and do so with integrity and excellence, as they serve themselves and all Beings.

All the areas of human endeavour listed above generate exciting Activities for people to undertake.

It is important to note here that the level of maturity in Consciousness of those who live in the New Communities of the New Consciousness Civilization, is such that many of the stipulations detailed above come instinctively, naturally and there will be no need to enforce them by law.

13

COMMON OWNERSHIP

As stated in the Constitution, as every Being on Earth has the right to be here and to enjoy freely and in equal measure the bounty and beauty of Earth, there will be things that Human Beings as collectives or as individuals cannot own but for which they have the responsibility to care for. These are things from which Human and all other Beings are meant to take only what they need when they need it, or are meant to share, for they are the finite and infinite resources of Earth, not created by Human Beings but gifted to all 'Beings' and therefore cannot be owned by Human Beings. These resources fall under Global Common Ownership and are held in trust by the Civil Services of the individual lands in which they are found on behalf of and for the benefit of those who dwell in those lands and for the benefit of all who dwell on and in the Earth. It is therefore the responsibility of all the Civil Services of all countries to make sure that all these gifts are properly managed on behalf of and to the benefit of all Beings dwelling on and in the Earth.

These resources are:

1)   all land and land formations on Earth;

2)   the seas and oceans of the Earth and all other natural bodies of water, whether flowing or stationary;

3)   all bodies of vegetation, especially large ones that are or should be recognized as having a global impact on the quality of life of those who dwell on and in the Earth and which have or should be given World Heritage status, e.g., the Amazon jungle;

4)   all natural resources mined/acquired from the Earth, be they from the land and land formations of the Earth or from the seas and oceans and all other natural bodies of water, whether flowing or stationary, all of which also qualify for World Heritage Status;

5)   the air we breathe;

6)   the environment of all Earth;

7)   the climate and weather of all Earth.

AN EXAMPLE OF HOW THIS WORKS:

A person who owns a prospecting and mining company has two choices that will enable them to undertake mining as their Activity:

1)   apply for a licence from the Civil Service to prospect a specific piece of land for the type of resources they have the ability to mine. In this instance, they may obtain the licence if:

a) the piece of land they wish to prospect does not have any environmental or World Heritage laws that forbid its exploitation;

b) the piece of land has environmental and/or World Heritage impediments whose requirements have to be met, and the company has the know-how and capacity, and depending on the complexity of the requirements, the proven record to meet all of them;

c) the company is state-of-the-art and therefore:

    (i)   has the capacity to prospect and mine at the highest standards required; and

    (ii) have contented highly skilled staff who are well looked after and who would therefore give of their best in this undertaking and not perform indifferently, or in some manner sabotage the undertaking; **or**

2)   they have to put in a tender in response to a call to mining companies from the Civil Service to prospect a specific piece of land for a stated resource. Since cost no longer exists as one of the main factors in considering tender submissions, tenders will be rated according to quality and capability of the companies. Therefore, the

owner of the company has to compete with others to prove that:

a) the company is state-of-the-art with highly skilled, happy, contented and highly motivated staff who would give of their best in the undertaking;

b) the company has the know-how, capacity and, depending on the complexity of the undertaking, the proven record to meet all the requirements of any environmental or World Heritage impediments associated with the piece of land to be prospected;

c) should its bid be successful, the company is in a position to proceed with the work and deliver results within the stipulated timeframes.

Neither the Business Activity owner nor their company will ever have the right to purchase or in some other manner own the pieces of land or the resources that they prospect and/or mine.

The same Common Ownership rules also apply to farmers. Farmers cannot own the land. They sign a lease agreement granting them the right to live on a piece of land and farm it for a specific number of years. The lease is renewable, and the farmer and her/his/their family can live on the land for the duration of life of the leaseholder. The farmer's child or children have to sign a new lease if they wish to continue farming the piece of land after the retirement or death of the original leaseholder.

Farmers no longer need to overwork, over-fertilize, over-chemicalize and squeeze the very last drop of produce from their land in an attempt to 'earn a living' or make as much profit as they can, and 'agri-business' undergoes a revolution as it sinks in that there is no financial profit to be made from its mind-boggling production methods, over-production and waste. Thus, the responsibility of a farmer in the New Consciousness Civilization is to:

1) produce produce that are of the highest quality, using methods that are in the highest state of harmony with the land and with the environment, supported by state-of-the-art technology. The land must be allowed to produce only what it can, following a natural rhythm that enables produce to grow to their full size and flavour and the land must be allowed to rest for periods that are the best for that land.

2) know and understand their land thoroughly and treat it lovingly;

Research will provide innovative solutions to the current practice of harvesting produce before their full growth and treating them with chemicals in an attempt to retain colour, shape and firmness by the time it is picked up by a customer, at the expense of full delicious flavour and perfume. Current knowledge and technology and new discoveries in agriculture make it possible to grow food in areas that traditionally would not support such an activity, e.g., desert areas. Amongst the recommendations based on some current possibilities could perhaps be the following:

1)   adopt and adapt the categorization of farming as large-scale and small-scale in as many Communities as possible;

2)   large-scale farming could perhaps concentrate on livestock, and crops such as wheat, corn, etc, that generally require large tracts of land. The produce from such farms are also ones that, with care and technology, can travel great distances well and so do not need to be harvested before their prime;

3)   small-scale farming would perhaps concentrate on vegetables, herbs, fruits and flowers. These are crops that can be grown on all sizes of land and generally do not travel great distances well. To reduce the distances this category of produce has to travel to reach the customer:

a) build communities around or close to small-scale farming areas, or vice versa;

b) encourage people to go directly to the farmer to obtain their produce;

c) encourage communities to have community farms where they can farm things such as chickens and eggs, vegetables and fruit;

d) encourage people to grow vegetables and fruits in their backyards or hydroponically in their homes or rooftops.

Thus, people are able to obtain food at their best and freshest state, as and when they need it.

Suffice it to say that there already exist many innovative approaches to agriculture based on honouring the Earth and those who dwell on and in her, that could be adopted on a much more extensive basis than they are today. Those pioneering these innovative approaches will be called upon to lead the revolution in agriculture in the New Consciousness Civilization. Agriculture therefore is another area that in the New Consciousness Civilization will experience exciting changes due to research, invention and innovation, to the great benefit of the peoples of the world and those who choose to engage with this sector as their Activity Beneficial to Society and to Self.

14

PRIVATE OWNERSHIP

In the New Consciousness Civilization, it is vital that you 'know thyself' and be able to claim ownership of your creations in order to be conscious Co-creators of Creation, of life and creator of your own reality. Therefore, in the pursuit of excellence in service to self and in service to all Beings, it is of great importance that an individual lays claim to and takes ownership of their work or idea, or business or invention, that has emanated from their passion, imagination, creativity and intellect. There can be no greater demonstration of love and no greater source of pride and joy than to joyfully offer the best of who you can be and the best of what you can create, freely to your fellow dwellers of Mother Earth and to joyfully receive and accept their best that is freely offered to you.

Thus, although there is Common Ownership of the gifts provided by Mother Earth to all those who dwell on and in her and although communities may own or be responsible for certain things by agreement, e.g., small-scale community farms, private ownership also forms one of the pillars of the foundation of the New Consciousness Civilization.

Private Ownership therefore forms a vital part of the New Consciousness Civilization. Indeed, every single person can own their own business Activity; they can own the production processes if they so desire – e.g., in the case of a unique product – but they cannot own the land, the natural resources or the sources of the natural resources they utilize to create the products of their business.

FIRST EXAMPLE:

1)   Anyone, eg. a baker, a performing artist, a jeweler, a shoemaker, a lawyer, a painter, can own and operate an enterprise. As owners, they have to shoulder the responsibilities of owning an enterprise, by meeting and maintaining the viability and standards of excellence requirements set for their particular enterprise. Equally, they have a right to claim ownership and recognition for the products resulting from their dedication and creativity.

2)   And so, for example, a shoemaker must endeavor to maintain the viability of her/his business through the personalized and caring service offered and stock turnover

and average number of customers served per specified period.

3) Similarly, however, if this shoemaker invents a particular process or tool or technology for making shoes, she/he/they are able to take out a patent for her/his/their invention in accordance with the laws that apply, if the shoemaker so desires. Or the shoemaker may in some legal manner claim ownership of her/his invention and then create an Activity in which they teach this invention to other shoemakers, and so raises the bar for quality of shoes and shoemaking locally, nationally or even internationally.

4) Recognition of this effort will come in the way of admiration, acknowledgement and local and national awards (as described in Chapter 12, Point No. 6), and even international awards, for excellence in service and for setting the benchmark for excellence in the industry.

SECOND EXAMPLE:

1) Those who own a business Activity that can mine/extract the natural resource from the Earth do so as their Activity and pass the resource on to the refiners.

2) Those who own a business Activity that can refine the resource do so as their Activity and pass the refined resource to the manufacturers.

3) Those who own a business Activity that can manufacture products from the refined resource do so and

pass the products to the bulk supply agents (especially for specialized goods) or directly to the public suppliers.

4) Those who own a business Activity as bulk supply agents and who then supply products to the public suppliers, do so as their Activity. Those who own a business Activity that then supplies the products directly to the public do so as their Activity.

Thus, every person who so desires can own a quality business as their *Activity Beneficial to Society and to Self.* They will be required to manage and maintain it to the highest of standards and the following will apply:

1) Quality is of paramount importance and business Activity owners have to provide the highest quality of products and services to consumers. A person is free to own more than one business Activity, but they all have to be legitimate, and they all have to offer the highest quality of products and service. There will be a general emphasis put on the fact that owning one business Activity offering top quality products and services and having the time to enjoy excellent work-life balance, is preferable to living a life of stress running several businesses of indifferent quality and service.

2) If a person ends up owning and operating several business Activities because they wish to manifest and experience their various passions, eg. the owner of a fashion line of elegant, made-to-measure clothes, also has a love of woodturning, creates beautiful objects made of wood and wishes to have both as a business, then this

person has to ensure that both Activities are viable and remain so. To that end they could find that they need the services of others to take care of certain aspects of their Activities. However, the business owner still has to meet at least the minimum required periods of hands-on as well as direct supervision management for each activity, required by law. Employment in such enterprises provide opportunities for those looking for part-time ABSAS, or for those who have no desire to shoulder the responsibility of owning and running their own business Activity.

Consistently under-performing Activities that do not improve despite every measure possible taken to rectify their situation, face closure.

3) It is the responsibility of business Activity owners to:

a) know every aspect of their business Activity thoroughly, with a direct, hands-on approach to managing it, as laid out by law;

b) provide and maintain a state-of-the-art environment for customers and staff, by providing the safest and most comfortable customer reception and activity areas; state-of-the-art equipment and tools relevant to customer activities; state-of-the-art equipment and tools and the safest and most comfortable work areas for staff to carry out the Activity; and state-of-the-art support structures at the place of Activity for both customers and staff;

c) take the initiative in researching ideas for continuous quality improvement and innovation;

d) consult with all staff on all major aspects of the Activity and on ideas for continuous quality improvement and innovation and on the implementation of those ideas to ensure an optimum environment for customers and staff and the legitimacy and continuation of the Activity.

It will be clear from the definitions of Common and Private Ownership that in many individual instances the rules of both will apply, as for example in the case of house ownership.

15

HOUSING

In the New Consciousness Civilization and according to an annual timetable, the relevant Departments of the Civil Service, e.g., land, housing, agriculture, fisheries, natural resources, etc., etc. collaborate to release to the public detailed information about:

1)   all the plots of land that are available for development; and

2)   all the plots of land that the Civil Service would like to put to specific uses

and requests the public to submit their ideas and proposals for the development of the available plots of land, as well as their approval, objection and counterproposals for the plots of land the Civil Service wishes to use for specific purposes. Based on all the information and advice available and on community needs and desires, the public has the final say on how each piece of land should be used, through the referendum process.

The Civil Service then puts out tenders for builders and developers to submit their proposals for the development of the land. As cost no longer applies, professional qualifications, skills, know-how, experience, invention, innovation and quality, i.e., the ability to source the best materials and technology that deliver, and the best, the most efficient and most environmentally sound use of the land, are important in winning a tender.

The full details of all the builders and developers submitting a tender are posted in the relevant section on the National Governance Website. Applicants will have time to explain their ideas to the public through Parliament and through specific programs via the various media outlets. Through the referendum process the public then selects the successful applicants.

In the case of residential property, members of the public then deal directly with the builders/developers to select a piece of land. They complete the leasing process with the Department of Housing and then work with the builder/developer to select a design for a house that conforms with the requirements of the piece of land and that meets as closely as possible the needs and desires of the houseowner.

In the New Consciousness Civilization therefore:

1) It shall be the law that every person must have a home, be that as an individual or as a family and every individual can have their own home once they reach the age considered to be the commencement of adulthood.

2) To ensure that every Being has a dwelling in which to live in comfort, an individual or a family cannot have more than one home and they must dwell in it. This may also mean that the plots on which houses are built reduce in size and double and triple-storey houses become the norm.

3) Every individual or family can own the dwelling in which they live, i.e., a house on a piece of land or an apartment, but as per Common Ownership laws, no one can own the land on which their dwelling is built. The land can only be leased. Therefore, in the New Consciousness Civilization and similar to what is the case today, there are:

a) houseowners – who lease land and build a home. A Houseowner is responsible for the upkeep of their house and the land. Responsibilities will be spelled out in the lease for the land; and

b) housedwellers – who lease a house only for a specified period. A Housedweller is responsible for the upkeep of certain aspects of the dwelling but the builder/developer is responsible for most of the upkeep of the dwelling and land. Responsibilities will of course be spelled out in the lease;

c) it is envisaged that most people would prefer to be houseowners rather than housedwellers and in the New Consciousness Civilization people will be encouraged to become houseowners and build a life and become stable members of their community;

4) What does 'ownership' mean in this context? It means that:

a) houseowners can build any type of house they wish, so long as the house complies with the building codes and all other requirements for the piece of land they have leased;

b) houseowners can stay in their house all their life if they so desire. They may renovate, expand or even reduce their house according to their needs and desires at any time they please, so long as they comply with the building codes and all other requirements for the piece of land they have leased;

c) houseowners have to live in a house they have built for a minimum of 15 years before they can completely knock it down and build a completely new house, or relocate;

d) if houseowners choose to relocate after living for 15 years in their home, the process followed could, for example, be:

(i) the lease on land, or both the house and land are terminated with the Department of Housing and the occupiers are free to become new houseowners or new housedwellers in a new location;

(ii) the Department of Housing offers the original builder/ developer first choice in deciding if they wish to take back the plot of land as is. If the original builder/developer accepts, they could:

- renovate the property and then advertise for a new houseowner or housedweller;

- demolish the house – permitted as the house would be at least 15 years old – ready for an interested houseowner to lease the land and have a new house built on it.

(iii) if the original builder/developer is no longer interested in the property, the Department of Housing adds it to their list of land available for development and it goes through the tender process, once again.

e) only in extraordinary circumstances – e.g., flood and earthquake mitigation works, civil construction works, state of emergency or any other imperative reason – and wherever possible after full consultation and agreement with the owners, will an owner be requested or ordered to vacate their dwelling and relocate either temporarily or permanently;

f) for sentimental reasons children may inherit a home from their parents. The lease for the land will then be transferred to their name and a new end date for the lease selected;

g) builders/developers must ensure that they set aside land on which they build housing to meet the needs of housedwellers, and lease, run and maintain these as part of their business Activity. Housedwellers are people who need housing on a short-term basis because they are, for example, foreign students who will return home at the end of their studies; are people who are in town on short-term work contracts; are people who are not yet ready to settle down, etc., etc.

5) Dwellings are built to the highest standards. State-of-the-art science and technology make it possible to utilize space as efficiently, effectively and environmentally friendly as possible, to create spaciousness, give the illusion of spaciousness and to maintain privacy. Some of the architecture and modes of transport ideas propounded by, for instance, Jacque Fresco in his Venus Project, and other modern-day pioneers of eco architecture and sustainable architecture, represent wholistic and exciting concepts and visions that can already be made use of in the New Consciousness Civilization. At a minimum, these ideas are a source of inspiration for architects who are up to the exciting challenge of incorporating environmentally friendly, new energy concepts and technology in traditional architecture and taking these to new heights or creating totally new ones. Universal Design Principles shall by law

apply in the construction of all environments, all dwellings and all buildings be they public or private, and in the manufacture and provision of all goods and services.

6) An individual or family that acquires a house on a piece of land must always look after the land either by themselves or by contracting the services of a gardening and landscaping technician and a very high standard of maintenance is required. As, in the New Consciousness Civilization the need to pay for goods and services no longer exists, no one has any excuse for not maintaining a high standard of cleanliness within and without their homes. With service and business Activities readily available to undertake the work, local Civil Service laws will require that homeowners properly maintain their lawns, gardens and fencing and wash down and where necessary re-paint the fencing, roofs, exterior walls and windows of their houses on a regular basis. Indeed, this will be a requirement for all buildings in the land, be they for private, commercial or Civil Service use.

7) Every apartment complex shall have a live-in manager with an office and staff on the premises, who shall be responsible for the maintenance and upkeep of the whole property, including the maintenance and upkeep requirements of everyone living in the complex, be they houseowners or housedwellers.

16

ENSURING FULLEST UTILITY AND ELIMINATING WASTE

As in the New Consciousness Civilization all 'Beings' are of equal value and money and all its values, systems and structures no longer exist, everyone can now acquire what they need and what they desire without any fear, anxiety or stress. This brings tremendous changes that are very far-reaching and positive to society. The resulting availability of time and peace of mind results in a tremendous reduction in disease; an explosion in creativity, research and discovery, invention and innovation and a love and respect for all Creation.

The assumption is that people who choose to experience the New Consciousness Civilization already possess a Consciousness that is mature enough to enable them to function in the Civilization with ease and grace.

However, depending on how the New Consciousness Civilization is created and established, it could perhaps be the case that for the first generation that embraces the experience, some of the realities of the New Consciousness Civilization could prove to be a steep learning curve and those spearheading the New Consciousness Civilization Movement, the Civil Service, the judiciary, private enterprise and the public will need to work closely together to quickly put in place those laws, regulations, processes, systems and infrastructure that will serve to eliminate or mitigate as much as possible the period of chaos and unbridled acquisition, hoarding and wastage that could perhaps result as the New Consciousness Civilization is phased in.

This would require a major strategy that would involve, amongst other things:

1) Establishing recycling as one of the major pillars of the New Consciousness Civilization in eliminating waste and ensuring the utility of all goods and services;

2) A complete overhaul of Planned Obsolescence regulations and the adoption of new measures by the manufacturing industry and by suppliers to ensure maximum utility of products;

3) Compulsory education and training programs that enable people to understand the difference between abundance and waste and how to enjoy great abundance and reduce waste to the absolute minimum.

17

THE DIFFERENCE BETWEEN ABUNDANCE AND WASTE

There is much that human beings can do to maintain a beautiful, pristine Earth and still yet enjoy much abundance. Humanity needs to understand and embrace a clear understanding of abundance that clearly shows the difference between abundance and waste.

Abundance means that you can always have what you require or desire to meet a specific need at the time you have that need, moment by moment, day by day.

For example, abundance means that you can plan and pace how and when you obtain food so that you eat food when they are at their best, which is what is best for your health. This means that you take the time to plan your menu and work out your quantities. You then pick up your groceries bag, use whatever mode of transport you wish and travel comfortably to a shop/supplier, fill up your groceries bag with the quality ingredients you require for all the dishes you wish to prepare, return home, go into your lovely, cheerful kitchen and cook enough lovely dishes of food in a quantity that will feed you and all those who will join you to eat until you are satisfied, in the lovely and tastefully furnished dining room of your lovely home.

There is therefore absolutely no need to go out and obtain huge quantities of food, simply because you can, but that cannot be consumed during the period when they are at their freshest or when they are at their prime, and which you then have to throw away because they rot in your cupboard. That is not abundance. That is waste.

In the New Consciousness Civilization reality, therefore, you have no need to worry about how you would afford the transport, the quality and quantity of ingredients and the cost of preparation of the food for that meal; nor would you have to worry about the next meal or about any other meal that you will enjoy as and when you need to eat. This means you live fully in the present and enjoy your life to the fullest, moment by moment.

As another example: unless you are a collector of vintage cars, in which case you will be encouraged to display them in a museum for the enjoyment and education of the public as well as yourself, you do not need to have 12 cars sitting in your garage doing nothing except having their engines warmed up by a Domestic Assistant every few days, all to little or no purpose, in order to prove that you are abundant or that you love cars. It could be that you have a large family and there will be times when you all want or need to go out together. So, all you require is a mini-bus or mini-van in addition to your own luxury car.

Another example, you do not need thirty-one dresses, with a different one for each day of the month, all of which you wear only once and then discard in order to get a different set of thirty-one dresses for the following month.

Such under-utilization of what are ultimately Earth's resources, is sheer waste, is not sustainable and results from a poor perception of what abundance is.

Human beings therefore have to be constantly assisted to develop in their human consciousness the mentality and attitude that enable them to always automatically take the paramount importance of the sustainability of Earth, its resources and the environment into consideration at all levels and instances of their decision-making. Every person is assisted in every way to gain an understanding of the need to maintain the interactions of climate, the environment, resources, alternate resources, waste, the natural life cycle of nature and the life cycle of man-made products, in as much balance as is possible and yet still enjoy great abundance.

Social attitudes, beliefs and expectations change as people develop new values and priorities in their life.

This obliges us to always consider whether we are using the Earth's resources in the best way possible. It motivates us to think, search, research, innovate, find and invent other ways of doing things. There is a tremendous explosion of new ideas, research, creativity, innovation, development and implementation of new technologies, new ways of controlling, minimizing or eliminating pollution, new sources of energy, new tools, new materials, new systems, new methods, new structures, new processes, the acquisition of new knowledge and the acquisition of wisdom that change our attitudes and beliefs accordingly, all of which bring tremendous and exciting changes to all aspects of human life and all to the good of the environment and to Mother Earth and all those who dwell on and in her.

It is one of the major responsibilities of the Civil Service and its Departments to encourage the populace in coming forward with their ideas and in assisting them fully to manifest and trial their new ideas. Once accepted as beneficial to society, it is the work of the Civil Service to then implement the new inventions.

Life on Mother Earth becomes a totally wonderful new adventure that births a new consciousness that births a New Consciousness New Energy Civilization.

As the New Consciousness Civilization is phased in, every person will attend compulsory training where:

1)   they learn how to let go of the fear of lack and the desire to hoard goods;

2) they acquire a thorough understanding of the new concept of abundance and the impact that this abundance has on human behaviour. For instance, as every person can now acquire new products of the highest quality, it is envisaged that the acquisition or exchange of secondhand goods will become practically non-existent. Thus, those who have a habit of acquiring products to excess and then dumping them in second-hand outlets after minimal use in order to get rid of them, will no longer be able to indulge in this wasteful practice;

3) they learn how to estimate as accurately as possible their daily, weekly, fortnightly and monthly personal needs without sacrificing personal freedoms of abundance and choice;

4) they learn how planning enables them to meet all their personal needs at the right time with the products, tools and services that they require and desire, thereby reducing waste to the absolute minimum.

On a lighthearted note, the old mantra:

> Use it up
> Wear it out
> Make it do
> Or do without

could be slightly modified to:

> Use it up,
> Wear it out;

If in doubt
Do without
You can be tasteful
Without being wasteful
Bless the earth
And she will be grateful;

then attached to a catchy tune and used as a lighthearted jingle, taught to school children, played in shopping malls, and on TV in the intervals between programs, etc, to help people learn to focus on what they really need, and when they really have the need!

HOW THIS WORKS:

In addition to the stock-take coding system, with each manufactured item having a shelf life assigned to it, certain items must also have assigned to them a 'minimum use' period during which time they must remain in use by the person who acquired them.

1) The minimum use period will particularly apply to big-ticket items such as:

- washing machines and dryers
- motor vehicles
- refrigerators
- deep freezers
- huge television/multimedia screens and systems
- motorboats
- caravans, etc.
- privately owned aircraft

These kinds of products must remain in use with the owner for a minimum number of years – just as an example, 3 years for cars; 5 years for washing machines – before the owner can hand in the product for recycling and acquire a new one. The Minimum Use Period for each product or group of products shall be determined during overhaul of the Planned Obsolescence regulations.

2) In the case of aircraft and as is no doubt the case today, experts in the industry, legal experts and the manufacturers will, through an international regulatory body, set the minimum-use and maximum-use periods for each type of aircraft. Very strict measures will be imposed for the manufacturing and maintenance of all aircraft to reduce to the absolute minimum the risk of accidents and loss of life due to errors in the manufacturing process. Increasing profit by offering instruments that are vital to the safe operation of an aircraft, as optional extras that only some can afford, becomes a thing of the past as all aircraft must by law be built to state-of-the-art standards, and cost is no longer relevant. Similarly, as air travel will increase greatly, training for pilots, air traffic controllers and other air transport personnel will be set at the highest standards possible, to lessen the risk of accidents due to pilot and other personnel error.

3) Infrastructure and services that are vital to the running of a nation will fall under the Common Ownership of the peoples of that nation, and the infrastructure, maintenance and compliance with regulations on a national scale carried out and maintained by the Civil Service on the people's behalf. The Civil Service, through tender, will obtain the

expertise and services of private enterprise to create, build and maintain, or advise in the maintenance of, national infrastructures and services. And so, for example, an individual/individuals may own a train manufacturing business Activity and through tender win contracts to build trains for the nation and perhaps participate in their operation and maintenance.

But the business Activity cannot then own the national rail transport system, or parts thereof.

Similarly, civil engineering enterprises can win tenders and build bridges and maintain them, in fulfilment of national transport development plans; but these enterprises cannot then own the bridges and control the flow of traffic over them.

4)   The same applies to air transport. It is advisable that a country has its own national airline, independent of private airline enterprises.

5)   Private individuals may acquire commercial aircrafts if they own and run an airline as a business Activity and they can do so to the standards of excellence required. Private individuals who have the qualifications to fly a commercial aircraft may also lease a commercial aircraft for a specific purpose that does not break any laws.

6)   Persons with a past criminal record will be required to undergo additional character tests before they are permitted to become pilots, own an aircraft, lease any type of aircraft, or own an air transport or travel business Activity.

7)   The acquisition of goods in quantities that are deemed beyond what are recommended as normal requirements, will automatically be assigned to the category of 'Business Activity' and will have to be acquired against a business Activity with a Business Activity Acquisition Card. For example, acquisition of more than say 30 dresses in one go or within a short period of time of a similar acquisition will be deemed as the acquisition of stock for a business Activity. The stock-take checkout points will be programmed to recognize such acquisitions and to switch to the correct mode. If, however, the customer indicates that it is for personal use, overriding the system to retain the acquisition as personal use will automatically trigger a reminder on screen and on the receipt that customers should please consider the environment, avoid waste and only take what they truly need at any time.

Continued huge acquisitions will be blocked at the point of acquisition until the acquirer can provide an acceptable explanation. If no reasonable explanation is forthcoming, the acquirer has to agree to once again undertake counselling to find out the underlying cause for this compulsion and undertake further education and training sessions on hoarding and on meeting all their needs and desires without incurring waste. For example, counselling may reveal that a person, who we will call Mary, who loves to acquire lots of beautiful clothes, also has a gift for, or some skill in, fashion design. By developing that gift and opening up a fashion business Activity, or by offering her skills to a fashion business Activity as a seamstress or tailor, Mary is able to satisfy her craving for the beautiful smell and feel of lovely new fabrics every day and so loses, or is able to control, the desire to acquire lots of new clothes all the time.

Suffice it to say that everything will be done to assist a person, for as long as they require it, to manage their lifestyle and learn how to enjoy abundance without waste.

8) The measures stated above are:

a) principally to control waste, as people get used to the fact that everything they require, and desire will always be available as and when needed and there is therefore no need for people to surround themselves with things that they really do not require and will never use.

Citizens respond positively because first-class structures are in place to support their efforts to change; to support them in their efforts to support others; to support society in looking after one another;

b) to, where necessary, enable inventors, innovators and the public to gauge the effectiveness/usefulness of a product and use public feedback to improve their product;

c) to enable the Civil Service to assess the needs and consumption of the people and therefore be able to assist the populace in meeting its needs;

d) to assist the Civil Service estimate what is available for exchange (trade) as accurately as possible. Goods and services are exported and imported on the basis that all 'beings' are of equal value and so items are exchanged based purely on need.

e) assigning shelf life and minimum use periods to products, maintaining statistical data on the acquisition/consumption of goods in order to enable the Civil Service and society plan and produce in an orderly and sufficient manner to meet the needs of society and for exchange will be carried out by the Department of ABSAS Monitoring and Assistance.

9) The only exception to these measures is when there occurs a 'quantum leap' leading to a vast change in a product, making it necessary to phase out the old product immediately or as soon as possible.

In summary, technology, invention, innovation, education and healthy changes in people's beliefs and attitudes will enable the successful attainment of the objectives discussed in this chapter.

There is nothing to prevent a person from enjoying variety and abundance in their life. It is simply that in every material thing that they acquire, they have to:

Use it up,
Wear it out;
If in doubt
Do without
You can be tasteful
Without being wasteful
Bless the earth
And she will be grateful!

18

RECYCLING

Recycling is one of the major underpinnings of the New Consciousness Civilization in reducing waste and will be mandatory by law. Cutting-edge research, invention and innovation turns recycling into a major industry with its operations integrated into every aspect of human endeavour.

AN EXAMPLE OF HOW THIS WORKS:

Every dwelling will have a recycling station consisting of a computerized state-of-the-art recycling system that replaces current garbage and recycling bins, making it easy for everyone to recycle all their waste all day every day. The different categories of waste will be transported by an underground conveyor system to recycling sub-stations where the sorting process is finalized, and the recycling process begins. The material is then transported to recycling stations where they undergo the various processes to make sure as little as possible is used as landfill, as much as possible is supplied to the manufacturing industry for re-use and the rest is turned into compost and supplied to farmers and the public in general.

Residents can have large items, such as refrigerators, deep freezers, washing machines, mattresses and beds, etc. collected for recycling by the providers of such services. These items will be scanned to ensure that they have met or surpassed their minimum-use period or have been tagged by a qualified technician as broken or outdated and beyond repair.

Appropriate recycling systems will be installed in all public and private buildings, public spaces and places and industrial concerns.

The recycling industry will provide the opportunity for people who are genuinely interested in the field to acquire new skills and careers as their ABSAS.

19

HEALTH

Health will be one of the areas of human life that undergoes tremendous change in the New Consciousness Civilization. A new understanding of health emerges as people come to realize that consciousness and beliefs play the greatest part in a person's total state of health. This new understanding leads to an evolution in the medical industry, based on a merging of spirituality, science and technology.

This realization about the important role of Consciousness and belief in creating a person's state-of-being, and in making possible the realities of the New Consciousness Civilization, enable the elimination of the serious mental, emotional and physical dis-ease that result from the very stressful lives we live today, and people begin to live long and healthy lives. It is envisaged that by the time a second generation grows up under the New Consciousness New Energy Civilization, the causes of many of the imbalances or dis-ease that make people lead lives deprived of their full capabilities – mental, physical and emotional incapacities due to dis-ease, malnutrition and neglect as a result of poverty and ignorance – should no longer exist and workplace injuries should be practically non-existent.

20

THE NEW CONSCIOUSNESS SCIENCE

I believe that it is important to reiterate here, under its own heading, the fact that one of the most important pillars that form the foundation of the New Consciousness Civilization is the **New Consciousness Science** – a science that fully recognizes and operates with and within Divine Consciousness; a science that fully understands that all things, absolutely anything that the Human can think up, can imagine, **absolutely everything, emanates from, are created with, and sit within Divine Living Consciousness**; that Consciousness that many call God the Creator; and that I humbly call *God The Eternal Infinite Living Void Of Consciousness.*

Therefore a Science that, as stated previously, is birthed from a merging of spirituality, science and technology, where scientists, visionaries, futurists and spiritualists all work together based on an understanding of Divine Consciousness; a New Consciousness Science whose protagonists therefore also birth creations that reflect Divine love, Divine beauty, Divine balance and Divine grace and that respects all 'Beings', respects all life; and that respects the Human Being as God Also.

21

PEOPLE WITH SPECIAL NEEDS

As stated in the previous chapter, a new understanding of health and the realities of the New Consciousness Civilization would eliminate many of the causes of dis-ease that we suffer from today.

Nonetheless, there will be people born with incapacities or who suffer injuries, e.g., motor accidents, sports and extreme sports injuries, who will have special needs, that will be met, in order that they operate as independently and as normally as possible in society.

Cutting-edge scientific research and technology could lead to the elimination or close to elimination of physical disabilities, as humans and other Beings become capable of re-growing limbs and other body parts, or of incorporating artificial parts into their body that perform as good as, if not better than, their missing biological body parts!

Universal Design Principles will be mandatory in the construction of all environments, all dwellings and all buildings be they public or private, and in the manufacture and provision of all goods and services.

22

DEPARTMENT FOR MATURE AGED AFFAIRS

Collaborating with all the other Departments of the Civil Service, the Department for Mature Aged Affairs is responsible for ensuring that all the needs and specialized care required by the mature aged are catered for and that all the support structures necessary for providing this care are created, put in place and maintained at state-of-the-art standards.

Given the freedoms, abundance and other realities of the New Consciousness Civilization, it is expected that people will live long, healthy lives and the retired and the mature aged shall be given every encouragement to continue living active, independent lives of travel and adventure, self-development, education and training, purely for the pursuit of excellence in service to self and, if they so desire, continued pursuit of excellence in service to all Beings through an Activity beneficial to society and to self.

23

DEPARTMENT OF VETERANS AFFAIRS

In the New Consciousness Civilization, war – and the commemoration of it - becomes a thing of the past and disputes are settled by negotiation and compromise in a restructured and empowered United Nations and by the rulings of a restructured and empowered International Court of Justice (as described in Chapter 41). In light of the Founding Principles and the freedoms and abundance of the New Consciousness Civilization, it will be a priority of the Department of Veterans Affairs to undertake research into new thinking about how to support war veterans in order to empower them to move on from the past and live healthy, productive and fulfilling lives in the present. It will be the responsibility of the Department of Veterans Affairs, working in collaboration with the rest of the Civil Service and with the public, to implement these new approaches together with all the support structures required, until there comes the day when the work of this Department is done, and the Department becomes non-existent.

24

OF THE PEOPLE, BY THE PEOPLE, FOR THE PEOPLE INSTEAD OF GOVERNMENT

The running of a country becomes truly of the people, by the people, for the people through a structure that is founded on and grounded in the New Consciousness Civilization's Founding Principles, *All 'Beings' Are of Equal Value: Consciousness and the Pursuit of Excellence In Service to Self and In Service to All Beings*, and the *Constitution for the Lands and Societies of the New Consciousness New Energy Civilization.* Thus 'government' and many of its roles and responsibilities as they are structured and practised today cease to have any relevance and are dismantled, while others change substantially.

In the New Consciousness New Energy Civilization, the basic structures that are set up to enable the people to run their country are:

1) The Civil Service;

2) The Role of Head of State;

3) Parliament (or some sort of forum).

NEW CONSCIOUSNESS CIVILIZATION CIVIL SERVICE DIAGRAM:

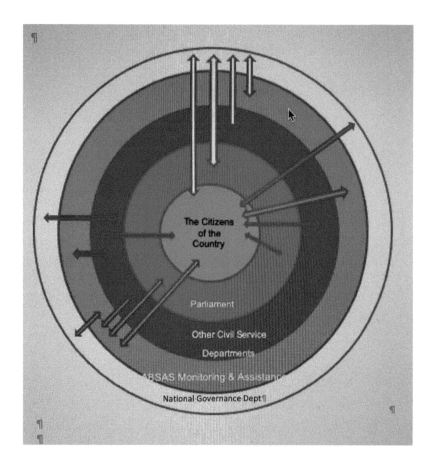

These structures exist purely to serve the people; to support and facilitate the day-to-day, short-term and long-term endeavours, objectives and needs of the people and their land.

The Civil Service replaces the 'Government' and becomes the major structure through which the people run their country. It also serves as one of the major sources to which the public turns for honest, clear and straightforward information and as such it plays a vital role in setting the tone for society.

Unlike many governments today, the Civil Service is not there to rule the people, to dictate to the people, to decide on their levels of poverty and enforce it. The absolute farce of elected government officials expecting, indeed demanding, to be praised by the public just for performing the job for which they were elected to office to perform, e.g., a vital road, or bridge, or safety zone, or school, or hospital or piece of medical equipment, are at long last provided for a community; or the callous disregard for human life and suffering as a result of botched or non-eventuating public service projects, due to bribery and corruption, are among the disrespectful and insulting behaviour that the public will no longer have to put up with.

The Civil Service is not there to deceive the people and promote in them a deep belief and feeling of helplessness and an inability to be in charge of their country, to take responsibility for their lives and to create and embrace change as a natural part and process of life. Too many governments, democratic and otherwise, play this ignoble role in the world today.

As stated previously and re-emphasized in other chapters of this book, the citizens of the New Consciousness New Energy Civilization are an educated citizenry that understand and accept the responsibilities of creating and running their own lives with honesty and with integrity, and they accept the responsibilities of fashioning and running their countries on all levels with a hands-on approach, with honesty and with integrity.

Every man, woman and youth are required to educate themself about local community, national and international issues. It is the responsibility of every citizen to know and understand the issues and so be able to make informed decisions about the matters that affect their lives on all levels, as, through state-of-the-art technology, every citizen is required to vote regularly in referendums on laws, regulations, policies, processes, systems, structures and the many other areas of human endeavour that make up the realities of life; and by doing so, are able to inform, instruct and guide their Civil Service.

Any member of the public with innovative ideas that relate to national civil infrastructure (e.g., roads, bridges, dams, airports, transportation systems, hospitals, research facilities, etc.) structures (e.g., office buildings, shopping malls, churches, mosques, statues and other edifices, sporting complexes, playing fields, parks and other recreational structures, etc.), environmental structures (e.g., artificial lakes and river pathways, forests, sound barriers, flood mitigation structures, catchment area basins and reservoirs, etc.) regulations, laws, processes, standards and all the other areas of national endeavour to benefit society, are requested to submit their ideas to the nation.

Through a referendum organized by the Civil Service the public gets to decide which ideas should be developed.

Persons with ideas that have been selected by referendum are assigned to the relevant Civil Service Departments where they and experts and those who believe they can contribute their knowledge and skill to manifesting the ideas, are all able to meet in the one place to research and develop the ideas. The Civil Service then organizes pilots to trial the end products before releasing them into society.

The role of Civil Service Departments therefore is to work with any and all members of the public to make all aspects of life better for society, the environment and Mother Earth. It is their job to work with the populace to gather facts and figures about society's needs and activities and plan and implement systems and strategies that meet those needs.

In the New Consciousness Civilization, therefore, the laws, regulations, policies, processes, systems and structures that underpin the many areas of human endeavour that make up the realities of life are invented, created, decided upon and developed by members of the general public from all walks of life, people with a pioneering spirit, visionaries, futurists, all working hand-in-hand with scientists and experts in every field of human endeavour, as well as those who have the skills and knowledge to turn visions into physical reality, and all of whom are willing to think outside the box and take a wholistic approach in achieving the objectives of the New Consciousness Civilization.

This inalienable right of every citizen to run their country makes it so that the societies of the New Consciousness New Energy Civilization will not allow the creativity and ideas that flow from the human heart, imagination and consciousness to become enslaved to any specific obligatory competing and supposedly opposing ideologies that are then imposed on the people as mandatory for running their country. Therefore, in the New Consciousness Civilization there are no political parties and there is no specific group in 'power' and others in 'opposition' with all the ridiculous farce that this system all too often descends into these days. Consequently, politics and politicians cease to exist.

As is enshrined in the Constitution, it is the right of all Persons to dissent, disagree and criticize any matter and when done in the public arena, mandatory that it is done with accountability, integrity and honesty and **always** accompanied by proposed reasoned alternatives that can be examined, and where necessary debated and voted on by the people. Dissent, disagreement and criticism therefore become positive catalysts for negotiation, compromise, change, invention, innovation, growth and evolution.

The societies of the New Consciousness New Energy Civilization understand that the '**ideal**' does not appear by magic. That standing in one spot and refusing to budge an inch, waiting for the ideal moment, the ideal situation, the ideal environment or the ideal set of circumstances, to present themselves in order to take action, or agree to move forward, based on acceptance of, or compromise on, current realities, possibilities and capabilities, leads to stagnation at best and suffering, chaos, destruction and self-destruction at worst.

With the experience gained through their fully hands-on approach in running their Societies, the citizens of the New Consciousness New Energy Communities are quickly able to tweak, change, improve and ameliorate systems, structures and processes to bring them closer and closer to, or attain, the ideal.

And even then, the ideal is not a static state-of-being! Like life itself, it is constantly changing, requiring changes in perception, beliefs and practices, that lead to the need for negotiation, compromise, change, invention and innovation, that in turn lead to growth and evolution.

With the inalienable right to run their country and the inalienable right to fashion their lives, a clear separation is made between the public rights and responsibilities, and the private rights and responsibilities of an individual, as laid out in the New Consciousness Civilization Constitution, the Founding Principles, and the All 'Beings' Principles.

Therefore, in the New Consciousness Civilization, it is every person's right and responsibility to ensure that the laws, regulations, policies, processes, systems and structures, that underpin the many areas of human endeavour that make up the realities of life, are in place and maintained in the land, in service to self and in service to all Beings, no matter their colour or creed.

Every person is free to live their life according to whatever creed they choose and to fashion their personal lives accordingly. However, adherence to and practice of religious, spiritual and other beliefs are strictly an individual's personal affair and has no bearing on the conduct of their public rights and responsibilities, in the proper running of their Communities and their Country.

Therefore, all Persons should make themselves aware that it is against the law, in the adherence to and practice of religious, spiritual and other beliefs, to conduct oneself in a manner that seeks to, or that directly, violate, deny, restrict, subjugate or eliminate any of the Founding Principles and/or any of the freedoms, rights and responsibilities of the All 'Beings' Principles and/or any of the freedoms, rights and responsibilities of the New Consciousness Civilization Constitution and of all other laws of the land.

Persons of like mind and beliefs are free to come together or live together in community. However, this is by each individual's own free will choice to do so or not to do so, as they choose.

Therefore, all Persons should make themselves aware that it is against the law for any Person or Persons to seek to impose religious, spiritual or other beliefs and practices on any other person or persons, group or groups, community or communities, state or states or the country, against their will and that in any way seek to, or that directly, violate, deny, restrict, subjugate or eliminate any of the Founding Principles and/or any of the freedoms, rights and responsibilities of the All 'Beings' Principles and/or any of the freedoms, rights and responsibilities of the New Consciousness Civilization Constitution and of all other laws of the land.

25

THE ROLE OF HEAD OF STATE

In the New Consciousness Civilization, the role of Head of State is not a single permanent position, to which an individual is entitled by royal birthright, or elected to as head of a political party that is in charge of governing a country for a specific number of years. In the New Consciousness Civilization, a country can be represented by different persons, in the role of Head of State, as it is a purely functional role. The process is as follows:

1) As one of its responsibilities, the Department of National Governance establishes an Office of Head of State that:

a) works closely with the rest of the Civil Service through the Directors of the Divisions of each Civil Service

Department and with Parliament, to ensure that the Head of State is fully abreast of all matters;

b) ensures that the public and the rest of the Civil Service are fully informed of all Head of State Activities, outcomes and matters arising thereof, as it is the public that decides, through the referendum process, the country's position on all matters dealt with by a Head of State;

c) provides all the necessary administrative support to ensure that the Head of State is fully equipped to carry out their function.

2) The Department of National Governance is responsible for conducting the process by which Heads of State are selected, and to that end sets up a Register of Heads of State comprising persons suitable to represent the country at the Head of State level. These persons are called Representatives and the process is as follows:

a) The Civil Service and the public submit through the mechanisms set up by the Department of National Governance, a list of functions of national and international importance which they have determined should be hosted or attended by the Head of State, or at which the country should be represented by a Head of State. The functions are categorized according to which Civil Service Department their subject matter best falls under and the list is constantly updated as new functions and events arise. Each category of functions also includes a selection criteria of the basic professional and other qualifications that those seeking the position have to meet;

b) Against each category of functions, the public nominates two persons they consider to have the highest degree of qualifications and knowledge for the functions in that category – e.g, breadth and depth of knowledge of the subject matters to be dealt with, fluency in foreign languages, high level diplomacy and negotiation skills, breadth and depth of knowledge of other countries and their peoples, etc., etc. – and considered to be of sterling character, to represent the country at that level. People can nominate others and/or nominate themselves;

c) This requires that the public do their research, be thoroughly knowledgeable about and keep abreast of, all matters relating to the governance of their New Communities at the local, community, national and international levels and those who step up time and again to propose ideas or solutions, or who possess outstanding knowledge and skill, all of which they put to bettering their communities, countries and the world in general. The public have to know and use all this information in their analyses as they indicate on a scale of 1-10 how suitable they believe each of their candidates to be, as they go through the process of shortlisting the candidates through the voting rounds of a referendum;

d) Persons can be nominated against more than one category of functions and can qualify for more than one.

However, each category can have only two elected Representatives;

e) The information is then collated and put to the public. Against each category of functions are the names of all the persons nominated, with full details of their biography, qualifications and experience, as well as their score. Each candidate's score is the average of all the scores received for that candidate, for that particular category;

f) Through the referendum process, and a fixed set of rounds, e.g., 5 rounds, the public elects their two Representatives for each function, whose names and other relevant details are then entered in the Register for Heads of State;

g) All persons who make it to the third round get invited to a grand function by the elected Representatives. Peers and fellow contestants get to meet and congratulate one another; new friendships are forged, new business relationships are forged, and all in a lovely, fun and friendly setting that promotes much good will.

h) Individuals who make it to the second-to-last and last rounds of the referendum have the potential to be called upon to join a Head of State's delegation for a particular function, for the following reasons:

   (i) they are regarded as having enough expertise, or specialized knowledge or training, to act as Advisors for a specific function;

(ii)   it provides an opportunity for citizens to build up their credentials for the position of Head of State;

(iii)   it is a positive way for the country to thank and reward the contestants for their hard work and dedication;

(iv)   it provides exciting inspiration and motivation for others, especially the youth, to give of their best;

(v)   the names of these Advisors are retained on a Register of Advisors that remains valid for the same duration as the Register of Heads of State, e.g., 3 years, after which new Representatives are elected, and a new Register of Advisors is created;

3)   All the elected Representatives carry on with their normal lives and Activities until they are called upon to represent their country as Head of State for a relevant function, e.g., a National function that requires a Head of State, such as for example a visit to the country by another Head of State; or an International function that requires the country to be represented by a Head of State, such as for example the signing of international agreements (with the exception of trade) between countries; or the visit by the Head of State to another country.

4)   The two Representatives for each category of functions take it in turns, starting with the most senior, to represent their country as Head of State for the duration of a function and through the period of debriefing to the public and the Civil Service back at home, after which the Representatives

return to their normal life and Activities, until they are required once again in their role as Head of State for another relevant function.

5)   The Representatives have to spend a certain number of hours per fortnight working with the Directors of Divisions of the Civil Service Department under which their category of functions falls, to ensure that they are fully across all matters relevant to their work.

6)   A Representative has no decision-making powers or other authorities in the Department to which they are attached, except for those that they may already exercise in the execution of the normal duties of their Activity because they were already a member of the personnel of that Department.

7)   Only when a Representative has to execute a function in the role of Head of State, can they exercise the authorities accorded to that role. And when in that role, a Representative can exercise only the authorities of that position for the duration of their role as Head of State. All other public authorities that they may normally exercise in the course of their normal lives and Activities, are undertaken by another Civil Service or other official acting on their behalf, until such time as the Representative relinquishes the role of Head of State.

8)   A Representative relinquishes the role of Head of State as soon as a function is concluded, as per the process laid out, and the Representative's right to exercise the authorities accorded the Head of State are suspended. They

may now exercise only those public authorities that they have the right to exercise in the course of their normal Activities and lives.

9)   A Head of State can call upon the expertise of another Representative on the Head of State Register for an Head of State Activity. In this instance the Representative accompanies the Head of State as a member of their delegation in the capacity of an Advisor and in that capacity does not exercise any Head of State authorities.

10) A country can have more than one Head of State representing it at the same time, at different functions that occur simultaneously. This is to ensure that the person with the best qualification in a particular function is the one who represents the country at that particular function as Head of State.

11) The Register of Head of State is valid for a specified period, eg. three (3) years, towards the end of which the Department of National Governance once again commences the process and invites the public to nominate and elect their Representatives for Head of State.

12) Although former Representatives can be re-elected to the Register of Head of State, this biennial referendum provides the opportunity for anyone in the country of good character and with expertise to represent their country at the highest levels. It provides a major motivation for the citizens of a country, especially the younger pioneers, to pursue excellence in service to self and in service to all Beings.

26

PARLIAMENT

From observation, it would appear that in the current civilization, Parliament or the equivalents of, tends to bring out the worst in people: behaviour resembling neglected chimpanzees in a derelict zoo; people ego-tripping on semantics, time-wasting tactics, contrived conflict antics based on contrived anger born of contrived passion; opposition mentality farce, breathtaking arrogance, immature and inappropriate behaviour, callous and selfish self-absorption, cheating, lying, stealing and other immoral and amoral conduct, and downright ignorance and stupidity and the irrational fear that is born of such ignorance and stupidity. Or perhaps it is politics that is to blame!

As politics and politicians do not exist in the New Consciousness Civilization, Parliament shall not only be a place of serious and civil discourse but also a fun and 'happening' place. Parliament is:

1)   first and foremost, the forum in which the citizens of the country present their ideas for the betterment of society to the public, as per the schedule laid out by the Department of National Governance, and from where it is then beamed out to the whole country via a substantial number of television and other media channels dedicated to the Parliament. Every day except for public holidays, members of the public who wish to make presentations can book parliamentary session times in advance. The program of presentations is published via the Parliament's media channels and updated in real time, enabling the public to attend or tune in, be informed and keep abreast of local, national and international matters, about many if not all of which they will have to take decisions by referendum;

2)   the forum in which members of the public, with clear detailed reasons and with accountability, integrity and honesty, can express their support, or their dissent, disagreement, opposition to, or criticism of any matter, accompanied always by proposed reasoned alternatives that can be examined, debated and, if necessary, voted on by the people. Parliament therefore plays the truly noble role of being a place where dissent, disagreement and criticism become positive catalysts for negotiation, compromise, change, invention, innovation, growth and evolution;

3) the forum in which the Departments of the Civil Service also first present their ideas for the betterment of society to the public, and from where it is then broadcast to the whole country; to be subsequently examined, debated and voted on by the people;

4) the forum in which the Head of State informs the public about Head of State Activities and outcomes and any matters related to these that will require a decision by the public via referendum;

5) the forum where the Departments of the Civil Service first present information of special national importance or urgency that must be noted or acted upon by the public;

Presentations can range from the serious to the lighthearted and humorous. They can take any form, from a simple speech to sleek multi-media productions, to storytelling, a documentary, a play, etc. What the presenters need to achieve is that the public stays fully engaged and fully understands the message or information by the end of the presentation.

This presents opportunities for the public to demonstrate a striving for excellence in the use of their imagination, creativity and originality.

This makes Parliament a dynamic place, a place where the public likes to go and where their attention is fully engaged as they educate themselves and give their opinion about the affairs of state.

Consequently, Parliament is a huge complex that allows for a large number of simultaneous presentations to the public. State of the art technology and the fact that these presentations are broadcast continuously and repeated through its many dedicated channels, means that people have every opportunity to see any and all Parliamentary presentations by following a daily, weekly and monthly schedule.

27

THE STRUCTURE OF THE CIVIL SERVICE

In the New Consciousness Civilization, the whole governmental system is overhauled, restructured, simplified, streamlined and becomes the Civil Service. The Civil Service is responsible for the day-to-day management of a country and its resources, working hand-in-hand with all members of society. Civil Servants ensure that at all levels of society, from local community to national, all infrastructure, structures, systems and processes – e.g., roads; bridges; dams; highways; railways; airports; seaports; energy, water and recycling systems, the stock-taking system, the public transport system, the national identity and education systems, etc., etc. – are built, put in place, are made to function as perfectly as possible, repaired or replaced, so that all are maintained at state-of-the-art level, for the comfort and benefit of its citizens.

Technology enables the Civil Service to become a highly efficient, lean performance machine, ready to carry out and attain the objectives of *All 'Beings' Are of Equal Value: Consciousness and the Pursuit of Excellence In Service to Self and In Service to All Beings.*

In the New Consciousness Civilization, the Civil Service consists of Departments that handle the major areas of activity of the nation, e.g., education, science & technology, agriculture, etc. Most Departments consist of 5 or more Divisions, as follows:

1)   A Directorate: made up of the Directors of the standard four, or where absolutely necessary more than four, Divisions of a Department. The Director of a Division of a Civil Service Department is a technocrat, visionary and futurist, highly educated in the area for which her/his Division is responsible and who works as a team with the other Division Directors to oversee the work of the whole Department. They ensure that the Department operates at peak performance to serve the people by making sure that its products and services comply with the decisions made by the people by referendum. The Directorate liaises and works with other Departmental Directorates to fulfill the objectives of the nation, which are founded on and grounded in the New Consciousness Civilization Founding Principles, the All 'Beings' Principles and the New Consciousness Civilization Constitution.

2)   A Development Activity Division: this is a very fluid and dynamic division as it is the division in every Department in which specific projects and products of the

Department, as approved by the public, are developed. It is also the Division to which members of the public, whose ideas have been chosen by referendum as being worthy of development for the betterment of society, are co-opted to work and bring their ideas to fruition. The proponent(s) of the ideas, supported by any required professional staff – eg. experts, engineers, technicians – provided by the other Divisions of the Department, become project teams who work to develop and create the products/systems/processes/policies and trial them through pilot projects before finally releasing the end products to the public. Once a project is finalized, the proponents leave the Civil Service and civil servants return to their normal duties until assigned to the next project. A highly educated technocrat heads up this Division;

3)   A Public Service Activity Division: this is a permanent arm of every Department that works hand in hand with the Development Activity and Policy and Laws Activity Divisions to ensure that at all levels of society, be that local, state or national, the projects and products developed by the Department, as well as all accompanying infrastructure, structures, systems, processes and procedures that are also developed by the Department, often in collaboration with other Departments and/or with private enterprise, are put in place and function as perfectly as possible; and that they are maintained, updated, upgraded or replaced when necessary. Through this process of implementation, maintenance, upgrading, replacement and recycling, the Civil Service maintains a continuous quality improvement cycle in all areas of

societal activity, so that all are maintained at state-of-the-art level. In addition, as stated above, the Public Service Activity Division provides expertise and support to all persons co-opted to that Department to develop their ideas for the betterment of society. A highly educated technocrat heads up this Division;

4) A Policy and Laws Activity Division: another permanent arm of every Department of the Civil Service that works hand in hand with all other Divisions of a Department and with other legal arms of the Civil Service to develop, put in place, review and update policies, standards, laws and regulations that pertain to the work and products of a Department and as these relate to the whole of the Civil Service and as these then relate to the laws of the land, that are founded on and grounded in the Founding Principles of the New Consciousness Civilization, the All 'Beings' Principles and the New Consciousness Civilization Constitution. It is the responsibility of this Division in every Department to constantly ensure that all policies, standards, laws and regulations relevant to the work of that Department are uncomplicated, streamlined, written in plain language and consistent within the Department and consistent with all other relevant laws of the land. It is also their responsibility to ensure that all members of the Department's Divisions are fully abreast of all current, updated and new policies, standards, laws and regulations in the performance of their work. A person highly educated in the legal profession, with other relevant qualifications, heads up this Division;

5) A Duty of Care & Personnel Wellbeing Activity Division: This is a permanent arm of every Department that is responsible for:

a) the recruitment of Personnel required for the work of a Department and the release of Personnel leaving a Department;

b) the total welfare – e.g., career paths and further education and training, work-life balance, health, workplace health and safety – of all Personnel of a Department including, for the duration of their stay, all persons co-opted to work on their projects in a Department.

A highly educated technocrat with other relevant qualifications heads up this Division.

28

THE DEPARTMENT OF NATIONAL GOVERNANCE

To facilitate the hands-on participation in the Civil Service by the public, all the Departments of the Civil Service, collaborating through their Public Service Divisions, set up the Department of National Governance, whose responsibilities are the following:

1) Establish, maintain and administer a state-of-the-art interactive National Governance Website that serves as the public face and a one-stop-shop for all the Departments of the Civil Service, with access to information, assistance and various tools to enable the public to easily carry out their civic duties in the running of their lives, their communities and their country. The Departments of the Civil Service work very closely with the Department of National

Governance to ensure that all the information, hyperlinks and tools are state-of-the-art, that they perform seamlessly and that they are updated in real time to ensure the greatest degree of accuracy. Therefore, amongst other things, the Department of National Governance has oversight of or direct responsibility for the following:

a) working in collaboration with all other Departments of the Civil Service, create and administer a section for each Civil Service Department on the National Governance Website that provides detailed information on the work of each Department as well as access to information, assistance and various tools to enable the public to easily carry out their civic duties in the running of their lives, their communities and their country. In keeping with this objective, the Department also:

b) hosts and administers the National Governance ABSAS Database, that is linked back to the master National ABSAS Database in the Department for ABSAS Monitoring and Assistance, to enable the public to access all relevant data, analyses and other information necessary to running their Activities Beneficial to Society and to Self;

c) hosts and administers the National Governance Business Activity Assistance Register, that is linked back to the master National Business Activity Assistance Register in the Department for ABSAS

Monitoring and Assistance, to enable the public to access help in running their business Activities properly;

d) hosts and maintains the National Governance Education and Training Database, that is linked back to the master National Education and Training Database in the Department of Education, Activities and Training, to provide people with detailed information that will enable them to acquire further education and training to progress in their careers, their Activities, or for self-development purposes.

2) Establish, maintain and administer the whole referendum process by which the public takes decisions for the Civil Service to enact. To that end, on the National Governance Website:

a) working with experts in the various relevant fields, creates and puts in place a National Electronic Voting System and its infrastructure to enable every citizen in the country to fulfill their civic responsibilities and vote regularly in referendums;

b) creates and administers the National Governance Inventions, Innovations and Ideas Database into which the full details of all submissions for the betterment of society are made easily accessible to every person;

c) working with experts, creates, puts in place and administers all the other tools, guidelines and administrative structures required for the referendum process, e.g., the National Governance Rejected Proposals Database.

Suffice it to say that in whatever manner hands-on participation by the public is configured, the emphasis shall be on:

1) enabling seamless interaction between the public and the technological tools of the New Consciousness Civilization and ensuring that the public can access, research and compare information, as well as submit proposals to the Civil Service with ease;

2) ensuring consistency and consistently high quality, up-to-date information and other resources are provided to the public;

3) ensuring that the objective of continuously enabling hands-on participation by the public in running their communities and country is achieved.

29

THE REFERENDUM PROCESS

The call for the submission of proposals by the public and the Civil Service on new and innovative ideas in, or change and enhancements to, laws, regulations, policies, processes, systems, structures and the many other areas of human endeavour that make up the realities of life in the New Consciousness Civilization, are made according to a timetable drawn up by the Department of National Governance, in collaboration with all the Departments of the Civil Service, and takes place on the first day of the first month of the year every third year, i.e. for example 1 January 2020; 1 January 2022; 1 January 2024, etc. This makes it possible for:

1)   the Civil Service and the public to have enough time to examine every proposal;

2) research and submit enhancements and counterproposals;

3) select the successful proposals through the referendum process;

4) develop the proposals;

5) pilot them;

6) incorporate further enhancements and pilot them again;

7) introduce them into society.

Naturally some projects will still be in progress even as new ones are being proposed, started or piloted. So, the citizens of the land will find that they are constantly engaged in the development of their society and country.

Specific months of the year are allotted to the different Departments of the Civil Service to put out an invitation to the public to submit their proposals, and so, for example:

- in January, the Civil Service invites the public to submit their ideas for all matters to do with health;
- in February, the Civil Service invites the public to submit their ideas for all matters to do with transport;
- in March, the Civil Service invites the public to submit their ideas for all matters to do with town planning;

- In April, the Civil Service invites the public to submit their ideas for all matters to do with building and construction;
- in May, the Civil Service invites the public to submit their ideas for all matters to do with the environment;
- in June, the Civil Service invites the public to submit their ideas for all matters to do with information technology;
- in July, the Civil Service invites the public to submit their ideas for all matters to do with education and with all laws of the land;
- in August, the Civil Service invites the public to submit their ideas for all matters to do with technology, innovation and new materials;
- in September, the Civil Service invites the public to submit their ideas for all matters to do with national and international exchange (trade);
- in October, the Civil Service invites the public to submit their ideas for all matters to do with agriculture;
- in November, the Civil Service invites the public to submit their ideas for all matters to do with natural resources and mines;
- in December, the Civil Service invites the public to submit their ideas for all matters to do with alternative sources of energy; etc.

8) The above is merely an example. Various considerations will be taken into account when assigning

the invitation month to a specific category of activity or industry and the benefits of holding specific ones consecutively.

9) There inevitably will be overlaps in categories. However, these overlaps enable the public to have more than one opportunity to submit an idea. For example, an information technology invention that can be used in education or health can be submitted to the Health Department during its invitation month, to the Education Department during its invitation month and to the Science and Technology Department during its invitation month. In each instance the originators have to and will be able to indicate on the project submission template the other Departments to which their information technology idea has been submitted.

10) All the information required for the submission of a proposal is posted on the National Governance website, together with project proposal templates that range from the quite simple to the quite sophisticated and automated, designed to elicit as much information about a proposal as possible, that will then be examined by the public, experts, visionaries, futurists, engineers, scientists and technicians.

11) Submissions have to meet the standard required and citizens may call upon expertise from anywhere and from the National Governance Business Activity Assistance Register, to develop their ideas to the standard required for submission. Given the resources available to everyone in the new realities of the New Consciousness Civilization, the public always has enough resources and time to submit

proposals of the highest quality – well researched, reasonably tested, detailed, very well assembled and very well presented.

12) Although the Civil Service will submit proposals according to the National Governance timetable, it is expected that a large percentage of submissions will concern national and international matters; thus, the Civil Service may also submit proposals at any time outside of the submissions timetable, with the necessary timeframes to enable the public to respond through a referendum.

13) Each Civil Service Department carries out a quick review of all the proposals as they are received, that deal with matters that fall under its own jurisdiction, to ensure that the proponents have followed the guidelines and used the correct templates for their submissions. Each proposal rejected outright at this stage is listed on the National Governance Rejected Proposals Database with detailed reasons for its rejection. At this stage, proposals can only be rejected for technical reasons, eg. the wrong template has been used, missing mandatory information, missing pages, attachments, etc., etc. They cannot be rejected at this initial stage because of the ideas proposed. That is for the public to decide as the proposal goes through the referendum process. Proponents are free to use the comments to amend their proposals and re-submit them before the deadline for submissions is reached.

14) Making use of state-of-the-art technology, each Civil Service Department downloads all the details of every relevant submission it has received, including those the

Department itself wishes to put forward, into the National Governance Inventions, Innovations and Ideas Database, making them easily accessible to all the Civil Service Departments and to the public. Those responsible in each Civil Service Department for doing so then prepare and post additional templates for the public to use to submit improvements or alternatives to original proposals. Proponents whose proposals were rejected in the initial phase are among those who use these templates to re-work and re-submit their idea. If successful, the original and rejected proposal is completely deleted from the Database and the newly re-submitted proposal joins all the others in the Inventions, Innovations and Ideas Database that will move on to the next stage of the process.

15) Proponents then introduce their idea to the public in Parliament. That, and through information and resources found on the National Governance Website, through conferences, seminars and workshops conducted at all levels of society and in particular at local community level, and through specific programs conducted through the various forms of media, in particular social media, the public, individually and collectively, is able to research and become informed, to discuss, to debate, to decide and to act.

16) Feedback from the public and from the Civil Service can range from outright rejection of a proposal and the reasons why, to suggestions for enhancements, to counterproposals or invitations for collaborative enhancing work where individual proposals can be consolidated to

create a stronger, more comprehensive and streamlined proposal. Given the resources now available to the public as well as to the Civil Service Departments in the new realities of the New Consciousness Civilization, all proponents always have enough resources and time to submit quality proposals – well researched, detailed, very well assembled and very well presented.

17) Similarly, when citizens object to a proposal, especially when it has a community-wide, nation-wide or international impact, their objections must not only be well researched, very clear and where necessary defensible by law or by the requirements of equity, fairness, humaneness and common sense, but in every instance they must also be accompanied by equally well-researched, very clear counterproposals for alternatives or proposals for improvements, that can be submitted for consideration in the referendum.

18) In a referendum composed of a fixed number of rounds, with the formula for determining the minimum number of votes required by a proposal to move on to the next round clearly indicated, in the interest of transparency, public vote determines which proposals are eliminated and which ones make it to the next and subsequent rounds. The number of proposals that make it to the final round is not fixed. The public through their vote determine which proposals make it to the final round and which are finally selected.

19) If in the final round there happens to be several proposals dealing with the same topic but which have totally different or conflicting approaches, proponents are notified and given a bit of time to see if any can merge their ideas before they are put to an extra round of voting for the public to decide which one should be developed.

20) The public is encouraged to make adequate comments (and what is considered adequate will be defined with examples in the documents) on the proposals they vote for as they make their way through the rounds. In every instance where possible, proponents are to be encouraged to provide as wide a variety of offerings through different versions of their products for the public to choose and use. The major exception to this is in national matters, e.g., infrastructure such as roads, railways, bridges, pipelines, communications, etc. where standardization must be maintained, and therefore reflected in all offerings, for the sake of quality, equality, fairness and efficiency. Where possible, owners of proposals use the comments they receive to further build, enhance and refine their proposals as they continue to progress in the referendum process, with the amendments clearly marked so that the public can pick up the new information quickly.

21) All rejected proposals are entered on the National Governance Rejected Proposals Database before they are returned to their originators and contributing material to the contributors, together with the comments from the public so that proponents understand why their proposals

were rejected. This gives proponents the opportunity to re-work their idea, if possible, for re-submission in the future.

22) To provide them with maximum resources and professional support, the proponents of successful proposals, together with any contributors, are co-opted into the Civil Service and assigned to the relevant Department where they are provided with a project team of experts, professionals and technicians who have the knowledge and skills to assist in developing the idea into a fully-fledged prototype.

23) The Department of National Governance coordinates the whole process, ensuring there are no duplications across the Civil Service and works to facilitate cooperation and collaboration within project teams and across the Civil Service, for there will be many instances where an idea will be developed as a collaborative project between several Departments.

24) The Civil Service now also puts its manpower to work to develop its own proposals that have been successful in the referendum process.

25) In every instance where possible the end products are trialed through a two-stage pilot program, with the results of the first used to modify and enhance the original proposals. A second pilot is carried out to ensure optimum standards and results have been achieved. The products are then released for public use. The owners of the product may refine and upgrade their product thereafter, taking into consideration any useful feedback received from the public.

26) Each Department of the Civil Service holds in safekeeping all the developmental materials emanating from the work of project teams that were carried out in that Department. The originators or inventors of the products may access these materials whenever desired.

27) The project is closed and owners and all contributors who were co-opted into the Civil Service leave the Civil Service.

This approach to the Civil Service empowers every person and ensures that they take responsibility for their own wellbeing, the wellbeing of their fellow citizens and of the whole country. It also generates new and exciting Activities Beneficial to Society and to Self for people to engage in and to follow their passion.

30

STANDARDS

Standards are very important measurement tools in the New Consciousness Civilization and are set at the highest level, i.e., at the maximum best that society, with its current and evolving consciousness, and its current and emerging knowledge, technological and scientific know-how, is capable of.

Therefore, in all the areas of endeavour that serve the needs of the public and the betterment of the individual and of the country, standards play a very important part in ensuring quality, impartiality, equality, accuracy, fairness and even justice.

To that end, each area of human endeavor establishes a professional body that has as its purpose to set the standards for its profession. All Activities are measured against standards and the standards are regularly reviewed and improved, as per the relevant regulations. So, for example:

1)   in the health and manufacturing industries and in the construction of infrastructure, standards are vital for maintaining accuracy, safety, quality and equality and ensuring that excellence is achieved through the utilization of state-of-the-art standards;

2)   in contrast to what happens currently in the world, individuals do not compete with each other but rather strive to meet or surpass the standards set for each activity. Thus, as examples:

a)   In the fields of education and training, comparisons are not made between students, or their past performance, or other similar processes, in order to work out a formula by which to grade them. If you meet or surpass the standards, you are certified as competent to the specific degree of excellence that reflects the results of your performance. This levels the playing field for everyone and makes for a much more impartial, accurate and fairer way of assessing performance;

b)   In most competitive activities that follow the traditional first, second and third formula, individuals pitting themselves against standards, with the hope of equaling or surpassing them, provide a more honest and accurate way of judging performance. This enables many more people to qualify and win in competitions as there need not be only one winner in each category, with judges forced to use dishonest tactics such as 'contrived conflict' in certain competitions to whittle down the field;

c) Even in competitive sports such as basketball, volleyball, rugby and soccer, greater emphasis could perhaps be put on the entertainment value – e.g., tricks in teasing your opponent, tricks in besting your opponent, tricks in balancing the ball, etc., in addition to besting the current highest scores in all aspects of the game, e.g., goals scored, attempts on goal, possession, etc., for a soccer match. This will encourage every player to concentrate on not only honing their skills and becoming good all-round players, but also adding flair and style to their performance and developing any other specific skills that they may have;

d) It goes without saying that for people with special needs, appropriate standards will apply.

31

EDUCATION

The pursuit and acquisition of knowledge, wisdom and above all, Enlightenment, is the most empowering and the most powerful thing on Earth, and indeed in all of Creation, that a Human Being if not all Beings, can gift themselves with. And it all starts with knowledge of Self and ends with knowledge of Self.

Thus, as stated in **Chapter 12**: the importance of honouring the imagination and its capacity to create, as well as the knowledge and wisdom that come from an 'inner knowing', from one's intuition, can never be over-stated or over-estimated, as they are the source and the food for human creativity and invention and innovation of the kind of education, science and technology required for the establishment, maintenance and evolution of the New Consciousness Civilization.

As also stated in Chapter 6: the citizens of the New Consciousness Civilization are an educated citizenry that understand and accept the responsibilities of creating and running their own lives with honesty and with integrity, and they accept the responsibilities of fashioning and running their countries on all levels with a hands-on approach, with honesty and with integrity.

Consequently, politics and politicians cease to exist. Every person acquires an education to enable them to engage individually in an Activity Beneficial to Society and to Self and every person is required to educate themself about local community, national and international issues.

It is the responsibility of every citizen to know and understand the issues so as to be able to make informed decisions about the matters that affect their lives on all levels, as, through state-of-the-art technology, every citizen is required to vote regularly in referendums on laws, regulations, policies, processes, systems, structures and the many other areas of human endeavour that make up the realities of life; and, by doing so, the citizens are able to inform, instruct and guide their Civil Service.

It is therefore clear that Education, like technology, is a major cornerstone of the New Consciousness Civilization. It is also quite clear that the consciousness of the young today simply does not connect with the old learn-by-rote methodologies of generations past. Children must also be allowed to have their childhood and not become straightjacketed in rigid education systems and left in the care of minders before they can barely recognize the voice, features and scent of their own mothers and fathers and bond with them.

Therefore, Education as it is currently understood and practised needs to undergo an evolution and become an experience where enlightened human consciousness and imagination meet and blend with enlightened pioneering science – the New Consciousness Science – giving rise to cutting-edge knowledge imparted through cutting-edge methodologies and tools. Education will therefore be one of the most exciting, dynamic and innovative fields of human endeavour in the New Consciousness Civilization and its management will require the services of courageous and dedicated professionals and visionaries who are true pioneers at heart. As is the case with all the other fields of endeavour in the New Consciousness Civilization, technology will play a major role in Education, especially since society will still have to apply some methodology to ascertain when people meet the standards set for the various areas of human endeavour.

The Department of Education, Activities and Training, working through its Area Offices, will be very busy indeed because its responsibilities will be:

1) to create and maintain the National Education and Training Database, which it shares with the Department of

ABSAS Monitoring and Assistance and the Department of National Governance. This database will contain:

a) the complete details of every institution of learning in the country and what standards they have to maintain;

b) everyone attending a tertiary institution of learning;

c) everyone undergoing training;

d) everyone going to school;

e) everyone going to kindergarten;

f) everyone undertaking home duties.

2) The Department also has full access to the National ABSAS Database created and maintained by the Department of ABSAS Monitoring and Assistance, if and when it requires information on the ABSAS of everyone else in the country.

3) Only authorized staff of the Department can update or amend records and the Area Offices can register citizens and update the central database.

4) All matters will be transparent and above board.

5) Since all work, aside from practical work undertaken at a laboratory or some other such activity, will be done on a computer, every student shall have a desk and a desktop computer at their institution of learning, as well as a laptop to access their study material outside of school hours or

when they are away from their learning institution. Consequently, all assignments and assessments, apart from the practical hands-on components, shall be done on computer and automatically submitted for evaluation. The results are automatically fed into the master database maintained by the Department of Education and the learning institution and the students access the results online.

6) Assessors must give detailed results and detailed explanations for the results they have given. This enables the student and their instructors to understand what the shortcomings were and enables the student to come away knowing what the correct answers should be. So, under every circumstance, the student is always learning.

7) Standards will be very important in the education system. Students of all ages come to realize that:

a) they are not in competition with each other;

b) they strive within themselves to attain or surpass the requirements of the standards set for whatever they are learning and to do the very best they can;

c) people have to be able to perform to the standards required in their ABSAS. You either are competent, or you are becoming competent or you change to something in which you are competent and which you like doing. You have to be able to perform to the required standards in your ABSAS;

d) there will be no point in people pretending that they have qualifications which they actually do not possess, and it will be practically impossible to do so because:

    (i)   to ensure the integrity of the process, no institution of learning can evaluate the work of its own students. The work submitted by students from an institution in one locality will be evaluated by assessors in another distant locality who do not know the students at all. Assessors will be physically present for oral, practicals and lab work and remain anonymous for all other assessments;

    (ii)   this ensures that the highest degree of consistency and standards in the quality of the education that they provide are maintained by all learning institutions in the country. All institutions have to constantly strive for excellence in order to remain relevant and turn out students who are of the same high standard as their peers in other institutions;

    (iii)   results are automatically assessed against the standards required. If you attain the standards, you are automatically certified electronically according to the degree of excellence of your performance;

(iv)   which assessors evaluate which institutions shall be according to a confidential schedule devised by the Department of Education, which is changed annually.

Naturally, new types of careers and occupations which we are not able to predict now will come into being and many current occupations/professions will cease to exist, such as accountants, bank tellers, tax agents, etc.

Education is one of the areas where a great deal of research, development and innovation are required to find the best ways for people to acquire wisdom, knowledge and skills. As education becomes available at all levels to every person in society and as humanity develops a new consciousness, the field of education will be a very exciting and dynamic area of Activity, and knowledge and the acquisition of it will become an exciting and multi-dimensional experience.

32

THE LAWS OF THE LAND

The main drivers of crime in society today are poverty, neglect, oppression, deprivation, a lack of a sense of self-worth, lack of education and lack of opportunity. Given the kind of spiritual maturity that enables a person to live and thrive in the societies of the New Consciousness Civilization, and given the opportunities, abundance and freedoms to be enjoyed in such societies, it is expected that crime would be non-existent.

The law-making bodies of the land and the legal profession are totally overhauled and undergo some of the biggest changes that society will experience in the New Consciousness Civilization in order to achieve the following objectives:

1) As money, finance and all financial institutions no longer exist, all laws of the land are systematically reviewed and all laws that pertain to this area of human endeavour are made null and void.

2) Every effort shall be made to simplify all legal language and to make legal communication as clear, as logical and as straightforward as possible.

3) By the same token, the study of the basic laws of the land will be compulsory for all citizens. This ensures that citizens know exactly what applies in their interaction with others as they go about their daily lives; and, as stated in Chapter 6, it ensures that the citizens of the land are an educated citizenry that understand and accept the responsibilities of creating and running their own lives with honesty and with integrity. The citizens of the land are an educated citizenry that accept the responsibilities of fashioning and running their countries on all levels with a hands-on approach, with honesty and with integrity. As such, people understand what the laws of the land are meant to achieve and can discuss, debate, decide and vote in new laws or amendments to current laws that are thoroughly grounded in the Principles of the land.

4) The law will no longer be based on precedence, which were based on the realities, attitudes and structures of human societies of centuries past. Instead they will be based on the Founding Principles of the New Consciousness New Energy Civilization, on All 'Beings' Are of Equal Value: Consciousness and the Pursuit of

Excellence In Service to Self and In Service to All Beings, the Constitution for the Lands and Societies of the New Consciousness New Energy Civilization, as well as on the realities, attitudes and structures of human society in the present and include justice, equality, fairness, equity and common sense and be decided by the people through informed discussion, debate and their vote.

The United Nations Organization, the International Court of Justice and the International Criminal Court will deal with legal issues of an international nature (as described in Chapter 41).

33

PATENTS AND COPYRIGHT

Patent and Copyright laws will be overhauled to reflect the new realities of the New Consciousness Civilization. In a civilization where money no longer exists, patents and copyright:

1) are important methods of claiming private ownership;

2) are a means of publicly acknowledging the brilliance, creativity, dedication and striving for excellence by an individual;

3) ensure that a person with a unique product as an Activity Beneficial To Society and To Self can own that Activity for a specific number of years, during which time the patent also acts as a motivation for the inventor to strive

for excellence and continually improve upon the product or even invent something better to take its place;

4)   in the case of products in general, act as a motivation for individuals to continue to strive for excellence through invention and innovation, either by inventing something new, or by replacing an already existing product should that product fail to meet updated required standards for utility and safety;

5)   in the case of creative works, also act as motivation for an individual to continue to strive for innovation and excellence in service to self and in service to all Beings;

Therefore, for example:

1)   for creative works or products of national importance, unique creative works, inventions and products resulting from unique designs, unique creative processes and techniques and uniquely created materials, patents may last from a minimum of say 10 years to the lifetime of the inventor;

2)   for creative works in general, patents may last from, for example, 5 years to a maximum of 15 years;

3)   for all other general products, patents will either:

4)   last for three years, i.e., the turnaround period for public submissions of ideas to benefit society; or

5)   until such time as the inventor(s) or some other person submits an invention that performs the same function so

much better that it renders the existing patented product redundant;

6)   Whichever is the longer of the two stated periods will apply, after which the invention enters the public domain.

Needless to say, top experts in this field will be requested to draw up this policy, which should be straightforward and easily understood by everybody.

34

ART IN THE NEW CONSCIOUSNESS CIVILIZATION

In the New Consciousness Civilization, every community will have a Creative Arts Centre with distinct spaces containing state-of-the-art facilities to exhibit the works of local and other artists in all spheres of art and to host conferences, workshops, seminars and classes by artists for public participation.

It is acknowledged that creativity is not something you can force but those who choose Art as their Activity Beneficial to Society and to Self, have to produce works to the degree required to make their artistic endeavours a legitimate Activity. Therefore:

1) Performing artists such as singers and actors, who claim their artistic works as their ABSAS, have a choice:

a) artists whose works continue to attract a certain determined number of attendees or more to their performances shall be deemed to be actively engaged with their Activity and their Activity shall be deemed to be legitimate; or

b) artists have to undertake and present to the public a determined number of performances per year. They may exceed this number but falling below it means that their Activity is no longer legitimate, and they have to take steps to rectify this; or

c) a combination of number of attendees per performance and number of performances per year. In this instance the target numbers shall be lower than that required for the individual processes. This combination allows artists a more natural rhythm and pace in their creativity and provides them the necessary flexibility in presenting their performances to the public;

d) performing artists also have to be prepared to put on private performances requested by members of the public but only as and when they are able. Large private performances can only be held in suitable public spaces or venues in front of an audience, or in a private but open space, e.g., in a park or suitably large garden and always in front of an audience. Community security personnel, i.e., the police, must be present at all times. Small private events such as parties with private arrangements between performing artists in the capacity of friends, held in one's home are not subject to this rule and are not considered in assessing the viability of an artist's Activity;

e) Performing artists may also reach their required Activity targets by teaching their art to school, college and university students, as well as interested members of the public.

Audience and performance targets will be averaged over the year to allow for seasonal differences and good and bad periods. Failure to meet audience and performance targets consistently over a two-year period will result in a notification to seek the assistance of an advisor or mentor to effect any changes necessary to bring legitimacy to the Activity or to engage in a legitimate Activity.

2) For visual artists such as painters, sculptors, potters, etc. who claim their artistic works as their ABSAS, the following shall apply:

a) visual artists have to produce a determined number of works and hold a determined number of exhibitions of their works, e.g., 4 art pieces per year, for the public to view and obtain, if available for acquisition;

b) members of the public can commission artistic works from an artist for their private pleasure – e.g., family portraits to hang up in a home gallery; decorative pieces for the house and garden and for the workplace. Therefore, in addition to their own creative works, visual artists have to fulfil at least 2 artistic works commissioned by members of the public per year;

c) the Civil Service will commission art works for civil service buildings, public spaces, schools and other learning institutions, and even as gifts for visiting and foreign dignitaries;

d) artists must, as part of their Activity responsibilities, be prepared to teach their art to:

   (i) the public in general through classes, workshops, etc;

   (ii) students in school and other institutions of learning;

   (iii) hospitals and other health institutions – for those with the necessary specialized training.

   These teaching sessions provide the artist the opportunity to educate the public about the meaning of their art pieces, the sources of their inspiration, the historical and geographical backgrounds and environments, where portrayed in their art pieces. In this way artists make art interesting at the same time as they give of their best to their fellow citizens.

3) Authors who claim the writing and publishing of original works as their ABSAS, have to undertake at least one of the following for their Activity to be considered legitimate:

a) publish a minimum of two original works per year; or

b) publish only one original work per year and undertake at least one other legitimate Activity, which could be from among the following:

c) also run a publishing business Activity;

d) be contracted to teach the art of writing in learning institutions, e.g., universities, schools;

e) run a business Activity teaching the art of writing to members of the public – through classes, seminars, one-on-one, etc;

f) mentor up and coming writers through seminars and workshops on different aspects of the art of writing;

g) hold readings and information evenings on the background of their books and explain the meaning of what they have written in their books;

h) edit the works of other authors;

i) undertake or be involved in the production of one or more of their works in a different medium, e.g., production of a book as a movie or a play; or

j) not publish any original work during the course of a year but undertake at least two other Activities from among the following:

    (i)   run a publishing business Activity;

(ii) be contracted to teach the art of writing in learning institutions, e.g., universities, schools;

(iii) run a business Activity teaching the art of writing to members of the public – through classes, seminars, one-on-one, etc.;

(iv) mentor up and coming writers through seminars and workshops on different aspects of the art of writing;

(v) hold readings and information evenings on the background of their books and explain the meaning of what they have written in the books;

(vi) edit the works of other authors;

(vii) undertake or be involved in the production of one or more of their works in a different medium, e.g., production of a book as a movie or a play.

35

CENSUS OFFICE

The Census Office will ensure that each and every person is registered. Consequently, they will also be responsible for the registration of births, marriages and deaths. Everybody has to carry an identification device that activates his or her access to everything in the society. Citizens are electronically reminded through their identity device of mandatory tasks/amendments/ renewals that need to be undertaken and the time limit on these. Past that date and they are shut out of all systems and will have to physically present themselves at the Department of National Governance to be sighted and complete the necessary reactivation process. Reminders will be sent at regular intervals right up to the last five minutes before shut-down. This makes it difficult for anyone to forget to update their contact details and all other matters and have these changes automatically made in all their records in the various systems. It is of utmost importance that all records are kept up to date.

Data supplied by the Census Office enables all the other Departments of the Civil Service in their projections and planning in order to meet the needs of the country and its people.

36

SOME EXAMPLES OF CHANGES BROUGHT ABOUT BY THE NEW CONSCIOUSNESS CIVILIZATION

As money and all its supporting structures and influence on society cease to exist, so will disappear a plethora of structures and services that are no longer relevant and that no longer serve society. For example:

1)   *Charitable Organizations* as currently structured will cease to exist. People come to realize that so long as they are of sound mind and body, they are responsible for and have to take charge of their lives; that they have every means at their disposal to do so and that they will be assisted to do so to the highest degree possible, through the many Lifestyle, Wellness and Wellbeing Coaching and Counselling Services that people, who genuinely like

serving society in that capacity, will train and get certification for and offer as their Activity to Benefit Society and Self.

Similarly, those who are incapable of looking after themselves due to an inability will be taken care of through specialized services, provided by people who have a genuine desire to serve society in such capacities and are certified to do so. For those who require it, their specialized care will be provided in specialized environments tailored to their needs.

Indeed, it is envisaged that in the New Consciousness Civilization the concept of family may change and the 'extended family' in some form becomes the norm. With the ability now to enjoy all one requires and desires – good nutrition, dwelling, transport, wellbeing and health care, lifestyle coaching and the services of lifestyle assistants, many elderly will live long, healthy and active lives in their own space within the family compound in an extended family situation, to the benefit of the whole family. Old people's homes become the exception.

2)   *Banks* will no longer have anything to do with money. Their vaults and safety deposit boxes become state-of-the-art secure storage to be used by the public to keep their precious belongings – e.g., awards and items of sentimental value; blueprints, plans and other such documents of original creative works; patented products or rare materials, e.g., jewelers may use deposit boxes to store precious stones and gold, i.e. materials that are not in

abundant supply and for which therefore demand is subject to a quota system or there are lengthy waiting times between ordered supplies.

The Civil Service may also use them to secure items of national and international importance, e.g., agreements, laws, national infrastructure blueprints and plans, etc.

3) *Insurance* will no longer exist in their current form, if at all. Due to technology, it will be difficult to lose personal items, but should that be the case, people can easily obtain a replacement from the suppliers.

In the case of international trade through WEACH, it could be that stockpiles of raw materials and commodities will be kept in all the countries of the world, each country selecting which raw materials or commodities it is best capable of stockpiling and maintaining to the standards required. The United Nations will have the authority to authorize the release of raw materials and commodities from the stockpiles, to WEACH to enable it to replace lost orders through its system. Businesses and institutions at the local and national level will initiate their claims through the civil service systems already in place in their countries for national and international trade.

Those with the scientific know-how will ensure that stockpiles are constantly drawn down and replenished so that the materials do not deteriorate and become unusable.

However, it is envisaged that the causes of loss and the need for recompense as described above will be rare occurrences in the world.

4) *Gambling Industry*: gambling becomes a harmless, fun activity with the thrill only in winning and besting your friends and opponents and earning a reputation as a skilled player, as you would in parlour games at home. The lack of any financial benefit may even have a positive effect on those who are addicted to gambling, enabling them to kick the habit, as an addiction often arises out of a desire or desperation to win money in order to become rich and abundant and in particular to settle debts and meet living expenses, all of which have become sources of great stress. Thus, in the New Consciousness Civilization, an addiction to gambling is no longer the downward spiral to doom that it is today. There is nothing to bet with, only your skill, your reputation, honour, acceptance and admiration by society as an honest and skilled player of the highest class, or ostracization by the gambling establishments and by society as a dishonest one. Gambling becomes an enjoyable pastime, a reason to dress up, go out and enjoy some pleasant hours with good friends and honest strangers, good conversation, good food and wine and engage in games that test your skills in a light-hearted pursuit of excellence!

5) The following are some of the things that cease to exist in the New Societies of the New Consciousness Civilization:

a)   taxes, tax returns and taxation departments

b) accounting, accountants and accounting firms

c) shares, shareholders, investors

d) automatic teller machines (ATMs) and cash registers

e) wages, salaries and bank accounts

f) loans, mortgages and rent.

37

NATIONAL AND INTERNATIONAL EXCHANGE (TRADE) AND THE STOCKMARKET

In the New Consciousness Civilization, the drastic reduction – and in as many areas as possible the elimination – in over-production and waste in the manufacturing industries as well as in all other spheres of life and human endeavour, is expected to lead to a substantial reduction in the constant demand for goods and in the consumption of the Earth's natural resources, as people adjust and learn how to properly meet their needs and desires by acquiring what they need only as and when they need it.

Thus, the exchange of goods between countries shall be based purely on need and, as is with everything else in the New Consciousness Civilization, does not involve money or any other financial instruments in any way, shape or form. Competing for market share, and production and labour costs no longer have any relevance and cease to exist.

The World Trade Organization is dismantled and instead a state-of-the-art World Exchange and Clearing House (WEACH) is established. Its job is to match acquirers with suppliers on a worldwide scale, based on data supplied to it by the National Stock Exchange in each country.

The National Stock Exchange forms a vital arm of a Department for National and International Exchange and changes to become the center for local and national exchange of commodities, resources and services in each country.

Technology facilitates the speed, efficiency and ease of every step in the process of local, national and international stock exchange.

1)   In addition to the systems of quality control that are put in place for all areas of human endeavour that meet the requirements and standards of excellence of the New Consciousness Civilization, highly trained professionals – Stock Exchange Inspectors – certified at the national and/or international level will be required to inspect commodities and products to ensure:

2)   that commodities, products, goods and services for national and international exchange, still attain or retain

the qualities of excellence that they should and that are required, and that no deterioration has taken place;

3)   that information on labelling affixed to commodities, products, goods and services for national and international exchange accurately describe the products they are attached to, their quality and all other relevant information; and that the goods match the original request;

4)   that all the necessary health and safety precautions in the handling, transportation and storage of all goods, and in particular dangerous goods, are clearly indicated and implemented, nationally and internationally – and not the case as it is today where reports keep surfacing about international/foreign companies dumping radioactive waste right beside local communities in 'Third World' countries, with the people living in those communities totally unaware of the fact that their death warrants have been signed for them.

(See: https://www.unenvironment.org/news-and-stories/press-release/bamako-convention-preventing-africa-becoming-dumping-ground-toxic)

The Stock Exchange Inspectors use state-of-the-art technological tools to carry out their work quickly and efficiently.

THE BASIC IDEA – NATIONAL LEVEL:

1)   The current systems by which raw and manufactured products are received from those who produce them and

supplied to those who consume them, will be reviewed, overhauled and streamlined by those who have the expertise in this area of human endeavor, to make the processes as simple and straightforward as possible.

2)   Through state-of-the-art processes, all Departments of the Civil Service keeps abreast of the state of supply and demand of commodities and resources that the country requires for the proper upkeep of its national infrastructures and services, as well as the national resources that the country can supply to others and it channels this information to the Department for National and International Exchange.

3)   The tracking and provision of information starts at the local ABSAS level where the production, supply, acquisition and consumption of raw and manufactured products are tracked through the National Stocktaking System.

4)   Activities liaise with Bulk Supply Agents to obtain the supplies they need to run their Activities and liaise with Bulk Acquisition Agents to hand over the end products of their Activities for distribution to consumers.

5)   The Bulk Supply and Bulk Acquisition Agents, and any other specialized Agents of Supply and Acquisitions, forward all the relevant data and information to the Department for National and International Exchange.

6)   It is first come first served as the Department for National and International Exchange posts all this

information in real time on the National Stock Exchange system and the matchup and clearing begins.

7) Through state-of-the-art technology the National Stock Exchange matches up all demands that it possibly can with supplies available within the country. The Bulk Acquisition and Bulk Supply Agents are automatically notified by the system and the details automatically transferred to another part of the system where they are held for a short duration to enable the Agents to check all details and agree to the exchange.

8) The Exchange Inspectors on the ground carry out their inspection to ascertain that the quality of the goods meets the required standards; that labelling and products totally match; and that the goods match the original request

9) As soon as agreement is indicated in the system, Agent, freight handler and transporter can follow the process for finalizing the exchange and for clearing and forwarding the products to their destinations.

10) Acquirers and suppliers whose requests fail to find a match in the country within 12 hours of being posted are automatically informed through the system and they have the choice to keep their requests in the system at the national level or have them escalated by the system to the international level – the World Exchange and Clearing House – to be matched up with requests and supplies from other countries. Processing is similar to what occurs nationally.

THE BASIC IDEA – INTERNATIONAL LEVEL:

It is only after the local and national requirements of a country have been met, or are being met, or will be met based on projections, that a country will then turn to the World Exchange and Clearing House, to either:

1)   Acquire commodities because the national production cannot satisfy local demand; or

2)   The country does not produce that specific commodity and so it is necessary to import it from elsewhere; or

3)   The country has an excess of commodities that it can offer to the WEACH to meet foreign requests.

NATIONAL & INTERNATIONAL STOCK EXCHANGE DIAGRAM:

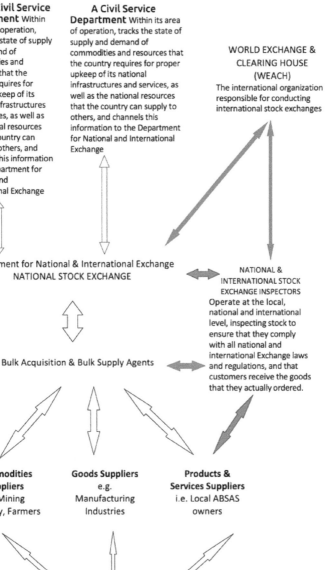

A Civil Service Department Within its area of operation, tracks the state of supply and demand of commodities and resources that the country requires for proper upkeep of its national infrastructures and services, as well as the national resources that the country can supply to others, and channels this information to the Department for National and International Exchange

A Civil Service Department Within its area of operation, tracks the state of supply and demand of commodities and resources that the country requires for proper upkeep of its national infrastructures and services, as well as the national resources that the country can supply to others, and channels this information to the Department for National and International Exchange

WORLD EXCHANGE & CLEARING HOUSE (WEACH) The international organization responsible for conducting international stock exchanges

Department for National & International Exchange
NATIONAL STOCK EXCHANGE

NATIONAL & INTERNATIONAL STOCK EXCHANGE INSPECTORS Operate at the local, national and international level, inspecting stock to ensure that they comply with all national and international Exchange laws and regulations, and that customers receive the goods that they actually ordered.

Bulk Acquisition & Bulk Supply Agents

Commodities Suppliers Eg Mining Industry, Farmers

Goods Suppliers e.g. Manufacturing Industries

Products & Services Suppliers i.e. Local ABSAS owners

Consumers

Thus, when any of the three conditions listed above present themselves, the National Stock Exchange system automatically directs requests to the WEACH. At the WEACH level:

1) Through state-of-the-art technology the World Exchange and Clearing House matches supply with demand and the automatic notification process is enacted through the system. The details are automatically transferred to another part of the system where they are held for a short duration to enable the Agents to check all details and agree to the exchange.

2) The Exchange Inspectors on the ground carry out their inspection to ascertain that the quality of the goods meets the required standards; that labelling and products totally match; and that the goods match the original request.

3) As soon as agreement is indicated in the system, Agent, freight handler and transporter can follow the process for finalizing the exchange and for clearing and forwarding the products to their destinations.

To maintain the impartiality and integrity of the system and ensure that countries honour the system and play their part in serving themselves and others with excellence:

1) It shall be an international law that countries conduct all exchanges through their National Stock Exchange and the World Exchange and Clearing House; and that countries have a legal and a moral obligation to also give in

order to receive. Therefore, countries that do not offer commodities or resources to WEACH in order that other peoples of the world can benefit from such bounty, cannot receive commodities or resources offered by others to WEACH.

2) As it shall be against the law to conduct exchanges outside of the National and World Exchange systems, there shall be no direct negotiations between acquirers and suppliers for the exchange of goods. Consequently, the traditional barter system in which specific goods are offered in direct exchange for other specific goods will not be allowed in the system;

3) Contravention or attempts to contravene the law shall be brought as cases before the United Nations or the International Court of Justice. Penalties would include exchange embargoes for specified periods;

4) The WEACH is bound by law to keep the sources of everything that is exchanged confidential in order to maintain the impartiality and integrity of the system. Should Stock Exchange Agents have any concerns about the quality of a product, they must raise that with the WEACH and with the National Stock Exchange who are the ones authorized to handle these matters at the international and national levels, respectively;

5) Should they be given or accidentally come by the information, Stock Exchange Agents are bound by law to

keep product source details confidential. Sloppy work by any of these professional services will incur penalties, leading to a bad reputation and loss of customers. An inability then to perform to the standards required to keep their business Activity legitimate means that they either improve themselves or give up that business Activity and find another. Therefore, it is important that people pursue excellence in their service to others in order to enjoy excellence in service to self.

Although financial gain and favourable labour and manufacturing costs no longer apply, where possible and where it greatly enhances meeting the standards of excellence requirements for an undertaking, manufacturing business Activities will be encouraged to establish branches or divisions of their manufacturing industries in the areas of the world where:

1)   they are best able to obtain the most important raw material(s) required for their product(s); and

2)   there are people, especially young people, who would be very happy to acquire state-of-the-art knowledge and skills and secure for themselves ABSAS they are truly interested in.

This could therefore be considered a win-win situation for all concerned as:

1)   collaborating with the Civil Service of another country to recruit and train personnel, obtain the natural resource, process the natural resource, establish the manufacturing

business Activity, supply local and national requirements and then make available products for exchange through the World Exchange and Clearing House, increases the ability of meeting with ease the standards of excellence required in all areas of such an undertaking;

2) to that end, the measures put in place to ensure sustainability, environmental safeguards, the avoidance of over-production, the quality of the end product(s), etc. could, in particular, greatly enable significant reductions in waste, as well as in the environmental impact of transporting raw materials elsewhere to be manufactured into end products;

3) state-of-the-art work conditions and environments for the personnel and the overall strategies for the pursuit of excellence in service to self and in service to all Beings also provide exciting and adventurous ABSAS opportunities for the citizens of the countries concerned;

4) all these measures taken together could perhaps also make it easier to ensure a steady supply of the end products to all markets – local, national and international through WEACH;

It is important to reiterate here that bilateral trade agreements between countries in a direct swap for goods is not allowed. All international trade must be done through the World Exchange and Clearing House where the rules of anonymity of source is always adhered to;

5) these kinds of collaboration enable positive and friendly exchange of knowledge and skills that can be put to other or further uses to the benefit of all concerned, for example:

a) other collaborative projects;

b) improved general knowledge and understanding of other peoples and their lands, leading to

c) genuinely much improved, or greater genuinely friendly international relations/ friendships and peace in the world.

All my discourse in this chapter is merely a simple example intended to convey the fact that:

1) With the elimination of money and all its ideologies, systems, structures, rules and regulations in the New Consciousness Civilization, trade is no longer an activity that is carried out as a means of earning revenue and income – and of earning them no matter at what cost. Trade becomes a totally free exchange of commodities, goods and services locally, nationally and internationally;

2) The first priority of every nation, therefore, is to use its resources to meet the needs of its nationals. Only when that is achieved, can a country offer resources to others outside its borders through WEACH.

3) The growing awareness and acceptance of the need to always consider the Earth and the environment, and the

changes in human attitudes and behavior that this awareness and acceptance brings, as well as the measures put in place to assist people in eliminating waste, all lead eventually to a reduction in the demand for goods, which in turn leads to a reduction in the volume of trade locally, nationally and internationally. Trade can now focus solely on meeting the needs of humanity, no more no less.

4) This New Consciousness Civilization reality eliminates the ridiculous and farcical acts and conflicts that are to be seen among nations today, as they fight over securing markets for their commodities, products and services and the whole nonsense of *carrying coals to Newcastle,* with countries producing the same goods and then trying to sell them to each other.

38

CUSTOMS AND QUARANTINE SERVICE

As with all other institutions, the activities of the Customs and Excise Department will be reviewed, overhauled and streamlined to reflect the realities of the New Consciousness Civilization. The areas of activity dealing with the imposition of duty or tax on imported goods becomes obsolete. Customs and Quarantine are fully integrated into one institution and emphasis will be on ensuring that:

1) all items are examined so that quarantine regulations are applied where necessary;

2) items considered illegal, dangerous or protected (endangered) are not trafficked and are properly handled;

3) all imported goods indicate Use-By and where relevant, Minimum-Use periods, or that goods that do not carry this information are assigned such periods. If a product is not registered on the national database, it is the responsibility of Customs officials to check with the Department for National and International Exchange to obtain this information. If Use-By and Minimum-Use periods have not yet been established, the process is commenced to assign these, through the Department which also liaises with the relevant international authorities for processing and finalization. A temporary period is assigned to the product in the system, which is automatically updated when the assignation process is finalized. The owner of the goods is then notified of the outcome.

Due to state-of-the-art communication and technology, the whole process can be done in a matter of mere hours.

39

INTERNATIONAL RELATIONS

With the disappearance of hostilities that results from competition, that in turn is a consequence of the realities of a world run on money, and with poverty, disease and stress rapidly now a thing of the past, the freedoms and abundances of the New Consciousness New Energy Civilization have a tremendous and positive impact on how people view and value themselves, their fellow human beings and the world.

People now find the time to enjoy their lives. People develop a genuine desire to acquire knowledge about the world and its peoples – their ancient philosophies, art, dance and cultural festivals. People enjoy the acquisition of this kind of knowledge as a pleasurable pastime.

Diplomatic relations begin to revolve around celebrations of national days and cultural events, international sports events; expositions and fairs; national and international achievements that demonstrate the pursuit of excellence in service to all; the celebration of international collaborative endeavours, e.g., major civil constructions by experts from several countries; multi-country transportation systems; space exploration collaborations, etc.

AN EXAMPLE:

Take the Commonwealth Games, for instance. Instead of hosting merely another mini-Olympics with predictable results every four years, the Commonwealth Games could have been and should be a major cultural and sports event that is used to showcase:

1)   the traditional/indigenous games of the countries that make up the Commonwealth;

2)   a cultural festival of dance, art, theatre, literature, fashion and food of the Commonwealth countries;

as well as the sports events that currently take place at the Commonwealth Games. Such a grand event:

1)   would be exciting and fun and would attract many tourists from countries that do not even belong to the Commonwealth. Athletes would be encouraged to take part in the indigenous games of other countries, even if only just for fun;

2) would have been, and perhaps could still be, an important avenue to preserve and promote certain cultural activities of value and enable them to evolve, as people begin to incorporate in them aspects of other events that they encounter, in order to modernize them, make them more appealing and more exciting to perform and to watch;

3) would also serve to wake up the world to the fact that there are many other types of games the world over and it is time to bring some of them into the international arena to add variety, fun and greater interest in current national and international games competitions. To that end, guest competitors reflecting Africa in Diaspora outside of the Commonwealth countries, other Countries of the Commonwealth, as well as athletes representing the Indigenous peoples of the world would be invited to participate.

If it is indeed the aim of this festivity to showcase the Commonwealth, then let it genuinely showcase the character and uniqueness of the peoples who make up the Commonwealth, even if the activities are limited to only sports!

The example given above provides people with the opportunity to promote friendly relations on all levels – individual, national and international and provides all involved the opportunity to pursue excellence in service to self and in service to all Beings in an enjoyable international setting.

On a more serious note, it is perhaps worth stating that there is no benefit to be gained and everyone stands to lose if some countries demonstrate an unwillingness to help other countries acquire the same state-of-the-art standards as everyone else. Countries and their peoples left to languish in an undeveloped or sub-standard state and attempts to engineer or perpetuate such an imbalance in the world will lead to the downfall of everyone, as:

1) undeveloped, under-developed and sub-standard environments cause environmental degradation, leading to global environmental issues, as we are already seeing today eg. droughts and famine, floods and famine. These will be a major cause of, or contribute majorly to

2) continued and increasing poverty, disease, suffering, despair and social unrest, leading to a state of war between those who are clearly enjoying the fantastic abundance and benefits of the New Consciousness Civilization and those who find themselves somehow shut out of it; leading to

3) major disruptions in the flow of commodities, services, knowledge and goodwill between nations; leading to

4) social upheaval everywhere as supplies and acquirers dwindle, Activities disappear and increasing deprivation coupled with excessively idle and discontented groups of people spill into social unrest everywhere.

However, this is a worst-case scenario that is difficult to see ever coming to pass, because:

1)   many countries in the developed world today are multicultural, with citizens coming from many other countries of the world. It is therefore to be expected that, with the freedoms and abundances of the New Consciousness Civilization, these residents or citizens with foreign roots would be very eager to see the people prosper in their countries of origin and would do their utmost to support their growth and development;

2)   energy constantly seeks resolution and therefore constantly seeks balance. The degree of maturity and balance in human consciousness that makes it possible to manifest the New Consciousness Civilization on Earth will not support such unbalanced attitudes.

Which brings us back to the Founding Principles; *All 'Beings' Are of Equal Value: Consciousness and the Pursuit of Excellence In Service to Self and In Service to All Beings,* and the *Constitution for the Lands and Societies of the New Consciousness New Energy Civilization,* and the need for everyone to make every effort to understand just how much they are responsible for their own lives and, as Co-Creators of life, just how much they are responsible for manifesting the realities of the New Consciousness Civilization and establishing it in their lives.

40

THE MILITARY

It is envisaged that the freedoms and abundance enjoyed by the citizens of the New Consciousness Civilization, the new realities brought about by state-of-the-art technology, innovation and invention and most of all, the continued growth and expansion of human consciousness, enable peace to descend upon the world.

The emphasis shall be on resolving whatever few international disputes and differences that arise peacefully through discussion, mediation and compromise. Cases shall be brought before a reformed and empowered United Nations, a reformed, expanded and empowered International Court of Justice and a reformed and empowered International Criminal Court (as described in Chapter 41). The decisions by these three Institutions shall be binding on all international issues.

The United Nations will continue to have an army composed of personnel from all countries of the world, primarily to keep the peace whilst issues are being resolved in the United Nations Organization or the International Court of Justice, or the International Criminal Court.

This is difficult to envisage, but it is perhaps possible but highly unlikely that the Communities that have embraced the New Consciousness New Energy Civilization, will continue to maintain weapons and armies for a time, until the generation changes and people come to realize that many disputes are no longer relevant; human consciousness expands to another level where the human mind, body and spirit change and so do their needs and humans discover their inner gifts and capabilities and become truly sovereign.

In the meantime, it is envisioned that as lasting peace descends on the worlds of the New Consciousness Civilization, armies will greatly reduce in size and an increasing percentage of those armies will not be trained for going to war. Their purpose will be to train and become highly capable in search and rescue and provide service in times of natural disasters – earthquakes, volcanic eruptions, tsunamis, hurricanes, cyclones, avalanches, forest fires, etc.

These special forces act on the national and international levels. Thus, at the domestic or local level there are search and emergency institutions such as the State Emergency Services who also receive state-of-the-art training and equipment. And at the national and international level will be the Engineering, Search and Rescue Special Forces.

Those who acquire special forces training but are retained in the reserves will maintain their skills and state of readiness by undertaking regular refresher courses, field training and field exercises with their special forces colleagues who are on active duty. Eventually all reserves will see active duty as they will be rostered on for a specific number of days of duty every month and as they are called up to replace colleagues who need to take a break from active duty.

All special forces and domestic forces not fully engaged in these specialized areas of Activity are expected to be engaged in other undertakings as well to maintain their full time Activity hours.

But even natural disasters will become rare occurrences as human consciousness expands and evolves beyond the dualistic games of conflict as a catalyst for growth. Armies will then cease to exist, and army training will simply become specialized training that people undertake who work in especially challenging terrain, e.g. geologists, engineers; search and rescue of people and animals out in wild and difficult terrain; instructors in the safe and proper training of people in extreme sports or survival skills, and training that ordinary citizens undertake simply because they wish to become and remain super fit and strong.

41

The United Nations, the International Court of Justice and the International Criminal Court

Given the realities of the New Consciousness Civilization, it is expected that much will change in respect to international relations and that international disputes and international criminal acts will become rare occurrences.

Given that from the individual right up to the national level, every person and every institution shall have the resources to meet their needs and to do the right thing, cases such as piracy; the dumping of poisonous chemical or nuclear waste on unsuspecting communities and their environments; modern day slavery; the opportunity and ability to hypnotize large groups of people – who most often are seeking an escape from the pain and suffering of their harsh realities – into committing heinous acts against their fellow citizens, shall all cease to be a part of human existence and rapidly fade into the past.

In the meantime, as society transitions from the old to the new and the realities of the New Consciousness Civilization and the continuing expansion of human consciousness transforms the human race, the emphasis shall be on resolving whatever few international disputes and differences that arise peacefully through discussion, mediation and compromise. Cases shall be brought before a reformed and empowered United Nations Organization, a reformed and empowered International Court of Justice, and increasingly more rarely in the case of individual crimes against humanity, a reformed and empowered International Criminal Court.

These three international bodies form the three separate but equal arms of the United Nations and are the three international bodies that will set international laws and international regulations and mediate and decide on international issues. All decisions by the United Nations Organization, the International Court of Justice and the International Criminal Court are binding on all international issues, although there are clear and robust avenues for appeal. Cases that would come before these three Institutions could perhaps be:

1) civil cases – e.g., disputes between countries, international disputes between companies or institutions, e.g., disputes over patents; spying on or stealing of

blueprints for new inventions; violation of the international exchange laws etc;

2) criminal cases – e.g., international criminal cases such as crimes against humanity; drug trafficking; drugs for weapons trafficking (crimes which as human consciousness matures, should all become things of the past);

3) international 'compensation' issues – if necessary and where possible, the replacement of resources for the re-manufacture of goods or products lost due to "Acts of God" or other accidents or disasters;

4) serious environmental damage caused by countries, companies or institutions, e.g., oil spills, nuclear accidents (with the discovery of alternative sources of energy, these too shall become a thing of the past);

All international issues are first reported to the United Nations Organization, which undertakes the preliminary legal work to sort out which cases go to which Institution and then forwards them to the relevant Institutions for their action.

To maintain impartiality, all decisions by one arm of the United Nations shall be reviewed by the other two arms of the United Nations to ensure that:

1) all avenues have been pursued to arrive at a just and fair solution;

2) all necessary legal procedures have been followed and that a decision does not contradict or nullify previous

binding resolutions or decisions, to the disadvantage or detriment of the party or parties against whom the case has been brought;

3) all necessary legal procedures have been followed and that the decision does not break any international laws;

4) where possible or necessary, the avenues of appeal are included and clearly spelled out;

5) in the case of individuals accused of crimes of an international nature, that due process has been followed before handing the case over to the International Criminal Court.

At the conclusion of this review and any amendments required, the decisions are announced and declared binding. All appeals and final judgements are similarly announced.

Therefore, all the current Divisions and activities of these three Institutions shall be reviewed in light of the requirements of the New Consciousness Civilization. Divisions, such as for example, the World Health Organization that may still have relevance in the new realities shall be retained and reformed. Others will be wound up and where necessary new Divisions created to meet the requirements of the New Consciousness Civilization.

It is important to reiterate here that the level of spiritual maturity and enlightened Consciousness of those who live in the New Communities of the New Consciousness New Energy Civilization, are such that many of the stipulations, rules and regulations detailed above and elsewhere in this blueprint, will either simply not apply, or they will quickly fall by the wayside and there will be no need to enforce them by law.

42

ESTABLISHING THE NEW CONSCIOUSNESS CIVILIZATION

How exactly will this unfold?

How exactly establishing the New Consciousness Civilization will unfold is yet to be determined, but it is hoped that new, exciting and innovative ways can be employed to establish a Civilization that intends to break all boundaries and that will definitely do so as it evolves. What is important is that:

1) the establishment of the New Consciousness Civilization is a joyful, fun-filled and in particular, inventive and innovative undertaking;

2) people bring a true pioneering spirit and courage to this undertaking; if necessary, feel the fear but do it anyway!

3) people reject the old, boring mantra about the incapacity of humans to change and instead recognize that change is one of the greatest gifts of life and should be embraced as such;

4) that people be willing to stand up and be counted, get educated and start taking full responsibility for their lives and the running of their country with a true hands-on approach;

5) people be willing and determined to make swift and steady progress, even as they exercise patience with themselves and with each other as they expand their consciousness to embrace this whole new way of living; this whole new way of 'Being'.

The following are just some thoughts thrown together about this matter that hopefully now and then bring a smile to the face!

A FEW IDEAS:

1) The New Communities of the New Consciousness Civilization begin as grassroot Networks that become a social Movement that spreads worldwide using the tools of social media in a very positive and effective way? Damanhur in Italy and Findhorn in Scotland are very good

and credible examples of how to go about establishing the New Communities of the New Consciousness Civilization.

2)   Or is it that the New Communities have to become a part of the system in order to change it, and so create political parties that contest and win elections and thus the mandate of the people to introduce the system?

3)   In other diverse and what is hoped will be interesting, fun and attention-catching ways, as detailed later in this chapter? Or

4)   In whatever manner the Creator, the Divine All That Is guides us to undertake this work?

The whole concept and system of All 'Beings' Are of Equal Value: Consciousness and the Pursuit of Excellence In Service to Self and In Service to All Beings, the Founding Principles and the Constitution for the Lands and Societies of the New Consciousness New Energy Civilization, encourage and enable people to go on an adventure in search of a new way of living, to think outside the box and even as you ask the question "Why?" you answer it with "Well, why not?"

As money and all its structures and influences will no longer exist in the New Consciousness Civilization, it is envisaged that anything up to fifty per cent of all the activities that people undertake today as a normal part of their daily life, and an equal if not greater percentage of the rules and regulations that govern our daily lives today, will disappear. Activities such as:

- waiting for payday in order to pay bills;
- paying the endless stream of bills that keep turning up at your front door!
- putting desired or required items on lay-by in a shop;
- tracking mortgage or rent payments;
- worrying about your investments in the stock market;
- paying for lunch;
- missing the bus or train because you need to add funds to your travel card;
- wondering how you are going to meet the cost of surgery or long-term treatment for an illness and trying not to believe that your only other option is to leave the earth;
- paying for petrol/gas at the station after you have put some in the tank although not as much as you really need to because of the cost;
- buying cheaper and tougher cuts of meat and second-rate products so as to keep within your budget;
- making sure that you keep your receipts for your tax return;
- preparation of your business accounts and banking your takings for the day;
- preparing and processing staff wages;
- emptying your savings account in order to purchase a new refrigerator and new tyres for the car;

- struggling to save enough to put the deposit on a mortgage for a house; or pay your way through college/university; or help your parents meet the school fees for your younger brothers and sisters;
- rushing to do all your morning chores of fetching water or firewood and then milking the cows before trekking 3 kilometers to get to school; a school which is held out in the open under a tree, or in an adobe hut classroom with few windows, a pit latrine for toilet facilities and one communal tap in the village square as the source of water for drinking, washing and bathing;
- struggling to do your homework by kerosene lamp or candlelight, etc.
- engaging in illegal activities and ruining lives in the process, in order to make money in order to survive.

Once the measures to be taken to render null and void all financial transactions, rules, regulations and laws and to remove money and all its structures from society, have been decided upon and written into the blueprint – the *New Consciousness Civilization Establishment Action Plan* – it will reduce the rest of the matters to be dealt with considerably.

Consistency in the implementation of the system is of paramount importance to avoid major problems and delays that could turn the whole exercise into a painful one for everyone. Thus, it is envisaged that the foundations of the New Consciousness Civilization will be phased into society in stages, one following smoothly but quickly on from the other, in such a way that they end up being implemented in an orderly manner but simultaneously for the most part, over a period of 5-10 years. As such:

Stage 1:

1)   In the Networks and Communities that are giving birth to the New Consciousness Civilization, people with expertise in the various fields of human endeavour step up to organize and coordinate the various activities that need to be undertaken by everyone involved in this Movement to start putting in place the systems and structures for the New Communities of the New Consciousness Civilization. For example: detailing and refining the Tenets of *All 'Beings' Are of Equal Value: Consciousness and the Pursuit of Excellence In Service to Self and In Service to All Beings*, as well as the *Constitution for The Lands and Societies of the New Consciousness New Energy Civilization*, to make them as comprehensive as possible; and commencing the detailing of new laws that need to be in place at the same time as the New Consciousness Civilization Communities are established.

2)   State-of-the-art technology and social media make it possible for the New Communities to communicate easily with one another, consult with one another, convene and exchange ideas and reach consensus, etc.

3)   Those with the specific expertise, including visionaries, futurists, scientists and experts in all the various fields of

human endeavour, as well as any other persons willing and able to bring a pioneering spirit to the task, all work together to draw up the *New Consciousness Civilization Establishment Action Plan*, which is a detailed blueprint for the implementation of the New Consciousness Civilization that is founded upon and thoroughly grounded in the Founding Principles, the All 'Beings' Principles, as well as the New Consciousness Civilization Constitution.

4) An Organization is set up to coordinate this work – *Organization for the Creation, Development and Establishment of the New Consciousness Civilization.* It is envisaged that the preparation of such a blueprint will take 2-3 years, given the wonderful communication technologies available today.

Stage 2:

Scenario One

1) The Organization for the Creation, Development and Establishment of the New Consciousness Civilization fully collaborate and support the local Networks in the various countries of the world, to develop into full blown Communities, using the New Consciousness Civilization Establishment Action Plan. These Communities exist alongside traditional communities on Earth but occupy their own space and live a reality separate from traditional communities.

2) These Communities expand as people outside of these Communities continue to elevate their consciousness and develop a desire to experience the reality of the New Consciousness Civilization Communities.

3) In this manner, the New Communities of the New Consciousness Civilization may eventually grow to entirely replace the traditional communities in a country.

Scenario Two

1) The Organization for the Creation, Development and Establishment of the New Consciousness Civilization fully collaborate and support the grassroot Networks that become a social Movement in the various countries of the world. This Movement establish a political presence and become part of the political system in their countries, in order to change it. And so, they create political parties that contest and win elections, and thus the mandate of the people, to establish the New Consciousness Civilization.

2) The Organization for the Creation, Development and Establishment of the New Consciousness Civilization fully collaborate and work hand in hand with these governments and use the New Consciousness Civilization Establishment Action Plan to assist them in drawing up detailed implementation plans for the phasing in of the system in their countries. These include the preparation of information and training materials for the public and for the Counsellors who will assist the public adjust to the new system. It is envisaged that this will take 2-3 years to

accomplish, given the technological capabilities and expertise that exist in the world today.

The establishment of the New Consciousness New Energy Civilization in the countries of the developing world will prove particularly challenging but also equally as exciting. For example, in Africa, the educated, entrepreneurial, innovative strata of society who currently enjoy the benefits of a modern lifestyle may face the same degree of upheaval as their counterparts everywhere else in the world. The real challenge lies in establishing the New Consciousness Civilization in villages and towns where people live and have lived a very traditional way of life with little change for many, many decades, if not centuries, and establishing the New Consciousness Civilization in such a way as to:

1) preserve what is beautiful and meaningful in the current and past way of life; and yet at the same time:

2) present new knowledge and methods and tools for verifying things that make it possible for people to feel comfortable in letting go of some of their old beliefs, superstitions and rituals that only serve to prevent them from enjoying the freedoms and abundance of the New Consciousness Civilization. The following quotation, attributed to the Author, Amit Kalantri, best sums up this idea: **"Mixing old wine with new wine is stupidity, but mixing old wisdom with new wisdom is maturity!"**

3) focus on:

a) communicating and working with the many resourceful, highly intelligent, innovative youth, many of whom have little or no formal education but who are a vast resource of invention and innovation, and enabling them to understand that they are the ones who have to be the foot soldiers of change in their communities, villages and towns;

b) assisting the youth, the young at heart and the many who are hungry for change to harness their energies and God-given talents, acquire discipline and focus and then providing the right kind of support, which in the majority of cases is all they need, to create a social revolution and establish a New Consciousness Civilization renaissance;

c) building the infrastructure, as well as the technological infrastructure all over each country as quickly as is possible and not just in the capital cities and a few large towns.

To state the obvious, the transition from the current civilization to the New Consciousness Civilization will be a steep learning curve for many of the current generation, be they in the developed or in the developing world.

However, I believe that as soon as people begin to understand that the, in many instances, painful and all too often impossible, struggle to live and make something of their lives will soon be over, many, many people will be eager and willing to jump on board and make the change. Added to this, and as I have already stated in **Chapter 39**, many countries in the developed world today are multicultural, with citizens coming from many other countries of the world. It is therefore to be expected that, with the freedoms and abundances of the New Consciousness Civilization, residents or citizens with foreign roots would be very eager to see the people prosper in their countries of origin and would do their utmost to support their growth and development.

In addition to the challenges already enumerated above, other challenges could be:

1) the potential for tremendous chaos as people realize that they can have any and everything that they require and desire. This will cause many to lose all control and try to acquire many things that they do not need or cannot use, e.g., 12 television sets, 15 cars, 60 pairs of shoes, 3 dinning sets, 5 sets of work tools, 14 lipsticks, 10 bottles of vitamin supplements, crates upon crates of alcohol, etc., etc. Many people will also find it difficult to resist the urge to hoard things out of fear that they may not be able to get those items in the future because they find it difficult to accept that many aspects of the way they used to live now no longer exist;

2) the potential for tremendous chaos as many people grapple psychologically with accepting the new reality because they have difficulty accepting or remembering that they no longer have to pay for anything and will try to pay

for things; or some suppliers may try to force people to pay them for their goods and services, fearing that the new way of living will not last and they will have to return to the old way;

3) the potential for tremendous chaos as many institutions cease to exist and their employers and employees are obliged to undergo a major process of change as they are assisted in finding and acquiring the knowledge and skills for other Activities that they find genuinely satisfying and that bring benefit to society and to themselves.

Based upon the New Consciousness Civilization Establishment Action Plan, the order of priorities includes the following:

1) Members of the public will be invited to train as Counsellors to assist people adjust to the new system. Training for the Counsellors will start with enabling the Counsellors themselves to adjust to the realities of the New Consciousness Civilization before they commence helping others to adjust to them. The Counsellors will:

a) assist people to understand the psychological impact of the new system; their own reactions to it; understand how the regulations that the Civil Service have put in place to control these reactions are meant to work and for how long, and how the individual is to use them to get in control of the new way of living;

b) work with the people so that they can begin to educate themselves and prepare for the decisions they will have to take regarding many aspects of the workings of the New Consciousness Civilization; and then assist people to start using and adjusting to the new systems as they are phased in.

Thus will also emerge exciting and fulfilling new Activities, professions and careers for members of the public who desire to undertake this work.

2) Commencement of a 2-5 year intensive educational and training program in which the citizens of a country learn about the New Consciousness Civilization and how it will work. Educating the public will take many forms:

a) extensive daily discussions and presentations in Parliament and broadcast on the Parliamentary media channels;

b) extensive and regular discussions, presentations, seminars and conferences broadcast on all media channels;

c) daily discussions, presentations, lessons, courses, workshops and seminars at every workplace, institutions of learning, community gatherings, commercial enterprises, shopping malls, cinemas, etc;

d) extensive and continuous distribution of information material both online and via letterbox or doormat drops, including surveys, questionnaires and forms for the extensive collection of information to enable the replacement and emplacement of the technological and other infrastructure that will be required in the community and in individual dwellings for the operation of the new system;

In addition to these formal methods, every effort shall be made to make use of fun and innovative ways to introduce the New Consciousness Civilization to society and to get the people well and truly involved in preparing for it and in phasing it in. Thus, there perhaps could be:

1)   public competitions; competitions held in schools and other institutions of learning;

2)   plays, films, dance, mime;

3)   art, storytelling, books, music;

4)   other new and innovative ways that people think of, create and present to the public or involve the public in;

5)   the greatest reality television show on earth – Shonda Rhimes, Netflix, Steven Spielberg, Barack and Michelle Obama, Oprah Winfrey, Richard Branson, Apple Inc, how about it?!!

Stage 3:

Establishment of critical infrastructure and commencement of the laying of the technological foundation of the New Consciousness Civilization will be phased in about a quarter of the way through the phasing in of Stage 2. By then, people will have had the time to understand that their country will be undergoing huge changes and already beginning to have an idea of what those changes will entail. It is vital that areas critical to the smooth and orderly running of society are transitioned and secured in the New Consciousness Civilization as quickly as possible. This inevitably means that changes will occur on several fronts simultaneously. These will be:

1)   changes that permanently remove money and all its related systems, institutions and values from the land;

2)   changes in law and to the laws of the land that establish, are founded upon and thoroughly grounded in the principles, objectives, rules, regulations and laws of All 'Beings' Are of Equal Value: Consciousness and the Pursuit of Excellence In Service to Self and In Service to All Beings, the Founding Principles of the New Consciousness New Energy Civilization and the Constitution for the Lands and Societies of the New Consciousness New Energy Civilization;

3)   creation and establishment of the new Civil Service structures that are founded upon and thoroughly grounded in the principles, objectives, rules, regulations and laws of All 'Beings' Are of Equal Value: Consciousness and the Pursuit of Excellence In Service to Self and In Service to All Beings, the Founding Principles of the New Consciousness New Energy Civilization and the New Consciousness New Energy Civilization Constitution;

4)   once again, it should be noted that there is already in existence today many state-of-the-art technologies that can be utilized as is, or quickly modified, to get the New Consciousness Civilization up and running quickly. The Leaders of the New Consciousness Civilization Movement, the Civil Service, private enterprise and the public will work closely together to put in place the laws, regulations, processes, systems and infrastructure as quickly as possible, especially those that will serve to eliminate or mitigate as much as is possible the period of chaos and unbridled acquisition, hoarding and wastage that could result as the new system is phased in;

5)   finally, it should also be noted that many of the rules put in place in the New Consciousness Civilization will be there simply to help the current generation maintain their balance and psychologically cope with the tremendous changes that transition from the current civilization to the New Consciousness Civilization will bring. As a new generation grows up with the realities of the New Consciousness Civilization as the norm, many rules will no longer be required and will fall by the wayside one way or the other.

43

CONCLUSION

We live in a time of tremendous change for the human race; a time when every Human Being needs to find a quiet place to reflect on their life, on the kind of person they truly want to be, on the kind of world they truly want to live in, and on the present. For, you create your own reality, and it is in the present that you create the future. In fact, the future is the present. It is this actual present moment. It is the decisions and actions taken right now in this moment ... and in coming to this realization and fully understanding it, it is the hope that we will all consciously take a stand for love, enlightenment, sovereignty, freedom, grace, joy, abundance ... and truly understand that these attributes arise from a love and respect for others which, most importantly, starts with and flows from a love and respect for Self – and for Self as God Also.

44

OH! ... AND JUST IN CASE YOU WERE WONDERING

.... how can someone who believes it is her mission to promote the philosophy for a New Consciousness Civilization that has moved beyond the need to use money and to help establish it, be charging for her book, and not only that, but also requires money in order to carry out this mission? Isn't that a major contradiction? Even hypocritical?

Well, ever since I wrote the first outline for this philosophy in 2006, I agonized and agonized for years over this same question, believing that I should reject money outright, believing that I should have as little to do with money as possible – that is, right up until August 2012.

That is when it suddenly came to me that: to be a miracle worker and change water into wine, you have to start with the water! To be an alchemist and change base metals into gold, you first have to have the base metals to work with!

Well, maybe not the best analogy since by all accounts only the Christ has been able to accomplish the former, and Saint Germain the latter! But you get the picture! In order to change something, you have to fully engage with that something. You have to know and thoroughly understand, appreciate and acknowledge with gratitude its purpose, then work with it to achieve wonderful new things!

As stated in my 'Foreword', money is Divine energy manifested in a physical form that has enabled it to act as a catalyst for human growth and evolution, by emphasizing the dualistic nature of life up to now – yin and yang, expensive and cheap, abundance and scarcity, the rich and the poor. This Divine vibrating energy, which like all things has its own type of consciousness, has done wonders for human evolution and has now taken the human race as far as it can go.

The human race now needs to release this Divine energy from its current form and its current role and allow it to be transformed and returned to Source. By doing so, this Divine energy also allows the human race to release itself and the many old energy systems and structures, and follow the evolutionary path to a New Consciousness Civilization.

There could not be a more Divinely loving and creative way for the Divine energy of money to set itself and the human race free and allow each other to evolve, than by enabling humans to work with it in great abundance to literally demonstrate the evolutionary process, by creating and putting in place the very systems and structures that set both the human and money free.

This publication, like its subject matter, is a work in progress and so will have amendments and additions made to it as we progress.

Blessings

Ronke

SHAUMBRA
INSPIRED